Mastering Plot

Mastering Plot

■ ■ ■

The Fundamental Structure of Fiction

J. Madison Davis

This is a work of nonfiction. No part of this book may be reproduced in any form or by any electronic or mechanical means including information storage and retrieval systems without permission in writing from the publisher, except by a reviewer, who may quote brief passages in a review.

MASTERING PLOT: THE FUNDAMENTAL STRUCTURE OF FICTION

Copyright © 2021 by J. Madison Davis

Lincoln Square Books supports the right of free expression and the value of copyright. The purpose of copyright is to encourage writers and artists to produce creative work that enriches our culture.

All rights reserved.

A Lincoln Square Book

Published by Lincoln Square Books

New York, New York, U.S.A.

www.lincolnsquarebooks.com

ISBN (paperback): 978-1-947187-13-9

Library of Congress Control #: 2021938710

This edition is a revised and updated from the 2000, Writer's Digest *The Novelist's Essential Guide to Creating Plot*

What the Critics say about books by J. Madison Davis

The Van Gogh Conspiracy

The Van Gogh Conspiracy is a sizzling ride, an adventure that ricochets through the worlds of fine art and 20th century history, carrying with it an iffy Van Gogh self-portrait, plus murder and double-dealing and intrigue, as it races non-stop across both America and Europe. The story is endlessly inventive, the settings finely etched, the characters people we can care about. A lovely read.
    Donald Westlake, MWA Grandmaster and Oscar nominee

In The Van Gogh Conspiracy Jim Davis gives us a clever plot, intriguing characters, and a down right gripping story. A genuine page turner!
    Tony Hillerman, MWA Grandmaster

Here's one you won't put down – an exciting international thriller with its roots in World War II. Let's hope it's the first of a series.
    Edward D. Hoch, MWA Grandmaster,

With his customary grace and insight, Edgar nominee J. Madison Davis crafts a taut tale of love, despair and theft in The Van Gogh Conspiracy, ratcheting up to a chilling denouement.
    Carolyn Hart, Edgar, Agatha, and Anthony winner

J. Madison Davis is a terrific crime fiction writer — smart, imaginative, a credit to the genre. His books always go on my 'must-read' list.
    William Bayer, Edgar winner

The search for a Mossad agent's father leads to a Van Gogh, a mysterious killer, and dark secrets of the Third Reich. This novel, itself, is like a fantastic painting. Bright, original and intense. A captivating thriller! J. Madison Davis is one of our best mystery writers working today.

    William Heffernan, Edgar winner

Begin with a Van Gogh stolen by the Nazis that turns up in Chicago, add a beautiful Israeli spy, an American Treasury agent, and various and sundry art specialists and/or killers and you get The Van Gogh Conspiracy, a wow of a thriller."

    Annette Meyers, author of Repentances and past president of Sisters in Crime

Law and Order: Dead Line (2003)

Author J. Madison Davis does an excellent job in capturing the feel of the show. Briscoe's sarcasm, McCoy's inflection, Southerlyn's "ice blonde" anger that's always simmering just below the surface... all are intact within these pages. The location and time that normally appear on-screen act as chapter separations, giving the whole novel the feeling of watching an episode.

    Knowbetter.com

Alfred Hitchcock in The Vertigo Murders (2000)

Davis (Red Knight) winds things up with a climax at Hitchcock's Bel Air home worthy of the Master of Suspense himself... With its tough-guy dialogue and minimal exposition, the text at times reads more like a novelization of a screenplay than a proper novel, but the slick execution and novelty of Hitchcock as sleuth will keep readers turning the pages.

    Publisher's Weekly

And the Angels Sing (1996)

Davis paints a harrowing picture of contained Nazism on U.S. soil. And in the Cleveland scenes he evokes memorably an era when American

big-city nightclubs were run by men with names like Charlie Mussolini, big-band players came on the stand red-eyed and "awash in the muggles," and the smoke in the room was "as dense as ocean water."
    Book World, (the Washington Post)

In this engrossing tale of soldiers, musicians and mobsters, singer Carl Walthers, "the Carolina Crooner," is on the verge of his big break—thanks to a Cleveland crime boss—when Pearl harbor is attacked.... Davis does not spring the crimes until halfway through the book, allowing Walthers and his fellow players to become fascinating, fully realized characters. When they are tested, their reactions ring true. The final chapter is bittersweet and memorable.
    Publishers Weekly

Mr. Davis knows the 40s well (his first novel, "The Murder of Frau Schutz," was a mystery set in a concentration camp) and he supplies this story with plenty of period atmosphere.
    Michael Harris, The New York Times Book Review

A well-written, highly entertaining novel, one well worth reading.
    Erie Daily Times

Davis has done a remarkable job re-creating the ambiance and events of wartime America, and his plot is both clever and entertaining. But the strength of his story is Carl Walthers, who is a perfectly imperfect Everyman. A fine read for mystery and history fans.
    Emily Melton, Booklist

A fabulously sooty tapestry of wartime nostalgia with its sour hero and multiple felonies a bonus.
    Kirkus Reviews

And the Angels Sing is J. Madison Davis' love letter to the era of big bands, gangsters and days when old ladies arose to give servicemen

their seats on buses. The most affecting sections of the novel are in the POW camp, where Carl learns that not all German soldiers are Nazis. But old-time Clevelanders will love the nostalgic look at the city when it wore its sinewy, blue-collar reputation with pride.
  Les Roberts, The Plain Dealer, Cleveland

The Murder of Frau Schütz (1988)

Very shortly after you begin to read The Murder of Frau Schütz you'll notice the little hairs going up on the back of your neck. That's not unusual if you read and enjoy thrillers, especially insightful historical thrillers. What is unusual is that reading this one stands them up and keeps them up....this book is a terror, as frightening when imagined as history as it is entertaining when read as fiction. What gives this book its edge is the considerable craft of its author combined with an unerring sense of drama and an eye for the gritty probabilities of bits of history we will never know.
  Frederick Barthelme, author of *Moon Deluxe, Tracer,* and *Natural Selection*.

First rate novel in the genre. Davis launches his tale at the right moment, from the right point of view, and shoots it through the turbulence of the end of World War II with pace, invention, and interest.
  John Casey, National Book Award Winner, author of Spartina and Testimony and Demeanor.

An exceptionally intelligent first novel....A rich sophisticated work. Well done.
  Kirkus Reviews.

A complex tale with a subtle moral message. This tautly written, multilayered fiction debut interweaves a murder investigation with one man's growing awareness of the horrors of the Nazi regime.
  Publishers Weekly.

A lot of good writing and plenty of action....a fine first novel from a writer to watch.
Toronto Globe and Mail.

This first novel by J. Madison Davis delivers everything it promises and more....Give it four stars and start reading.
New York Daily News.

Accurate detail, believable characters, skillfully handled dialogue and a tense plot place his tale a generous cut above the customary World War II novel.
Houston Post

A damn good read... Engrossing. A suspenseful psychological thriller.
Parnell Hall, author of Detective and Favor.

... what an extraordinary and unusual story you have created and how tremendously impressed am I by it. It's so completely different from any other novel I've read, it scarcely comes under the heading of crime novel: it's totally original.
Susan Moody, author of Playing with Fire, and the Penny Wanawake series.

Pick this up when you have a cold, winter night, a good fire going and plenty of time because once you start The Murder of Frau Schütz, you won't want to put it down.... an impressive, well-crafted first novel.
Houston Chronicle.

Compelling.... Davis avoids the clichés and formula writing that so often plague the detective genre. Instead he pushes the novel into the ranks of fine fiction by exploring the complexities of human existence within the Nazi regime.
The New Letters Review of Books.

Unusually subtle.... The real virtues, though, lie in the skill in which Davis engages us in his hero, withour ever letting us forget Nazi viciousness and degradation.
    Chicago Tribune

That this is a first novel is absolutely astonishing. Davis has come up with a superb plot and he combines that with great narrative skills this is a page-turner.
    Erie Daily Times.

A masterful commentary on the state of mind that led the German people to allow the Holocaust to happen.... Altogether it is a fascinating and chilling piece of fiction.
    St. Petersburg Times.

Ingenious...[Davis] plays the old game in a fresh new way.
    Joseph Wambaugh, author of The Secrets of Harry Bright, The Golden Orange, and The Onion Field.

Red Knight (1992)

Multifaceted characters and solid plotting make Red Knight an entertaining addition to a promising p.i. series.
    Booklist

This peculiarly appealing New Orleans mystery offers twice the pleasure of a hot beignet.
    Publishers Weekly

What's becoming increasingly clear as the books roll out is that J. Madison Davis is a master of complex, highly inventive plotting.
    Erie Daily Times

You will get caught up in the fast and furious life style of the many colorful yet dubious characters as the story comes to a surprise but grim ending. Great mystery.
    Rendezvous

Bloody Marko (1991)

A sophisticated story well told. Rattles in the brain for weeks.
    Kirkus Reviews

With insight and sensitivity, Davis takes on a difficult subject,… this is a provocative portrait of a man profoundly influenced by his time and place.
    Publishers Weekly

Thoughtful… powerful and suspenseful. The author, a superb writer, graphically describes the pitiless horrors facing these desperate people as they fight against the vastly superior Nazi legions.
    Newgate Callendar
    New York Times Book Review

Bloody Marko is a well-structured book, a remarkable exercise in peeling back layer after layer of a man's character, and Davis' clear, compelling prose is up to the job.
    Drood Review

J. Madison Davis has produced a powerful tour de force….Bloody Marko is a novel about human purpose, human cruelty, human stupidity; and about love, hate, and helplessness. It is compelling, fascinating, and disturbing.
    Richard Langford
    Deland (Fl.) Sun News

White Rook (1990)

J. Madison Davis has a knack for choosing fascinating milieus and creating compelling characters. His work is becoming ever sleeker and more innovative. He is a welcome new voice in the world of mystery fiction.

Gerald Petievich, author of To Live and Die in L. A., Shakedown, and Earth Angels.

This is a spellbinding thriller, too close to real subversive threats for comfort.

Publishers Weekly.

… a remarkable and powerful novel. You're an original, my dear sir, and must have confounded any number of critics/librarians/booksellers and others in the business of categorizing literature. For you are a writer with an armory full of unexpected weapons and no respecter of conventional modes of story-telling …. It's not easy to combine seriousness of purpose and enviable intellectual integrity with tolerant humanity, elegant wit and generous humor. Still rarer and more precious in an author is the ability to construct a frighteningly plausible plot, build up terrific narrative pace and still people a story with fully rounded, credible characters with minds of their own.

James Melville, author of The Reluctant Ronin, Kimono for a Corpse, and others of the Superintendent Otani series

A powerful novel exploring the bigotry within us all.

The Bloomsbury Review.

This fully rounded character [Dub Greenert] with his offbeat, well-written romance, together with the incendiary subject matter, combine for a memorable fiction.

Cumberland (Md.) Times-News

Dick Francis (1989)

The first book-length study of Dick Francis ....Recommended.
   Choice.

We learn a great deal about an author who is clearly one of Britain's and America's favorites...valuable and welcome.
   Clues.

Conversations with Robertson Davies (1989)

Witty, erudite, and thoughtful those attributes are everywhere evident in this fascinating collection.
   Booklist.

Robertson Davies springs from these pages as an expansive, erudite, and playful intellect, as willing to explore new ideas as he is to rediscuss old ones.
   Toronto Star.

An interesting and entertaining book to read and a valuable source for future reference.
   Books in Canada.

Judicious editorial selection by J. Madison Davis.
   New York Times.

Amusing and thoughtful.
   University Press Book News.

Murderous Schemes (1996)
   Donald Westlake, ed.; J. Madison Davis, contributing ed.

What is this drug anyway? Westlake asks about the timeless attraction of detective stories. This anthology answers by breaking the

genre into eight types, each illustrated by four splendid examples. Sensible analyses.
    Publishers Weekly

The best book of its kind this year.
    Wall Street Journal

The Shakespeare Name Dictionary (1996)
    J. Madison Davis and A. Daniel Frankforter

The Dictionary, a valuable addition to the seemingly saturated field of Shakespeare reference, explains it all in engaging, informative articles.
    Wilson Library Bulletin

Davis and Frankforter list every name, proper adjective, official title, literary and musical title, and place names appearing in Shakespeare's plays and poems. Packed with information, recommended for all levels.
    Choice

Table of Contents

Introduction: Becoming A Better Writer · · · · · · · · · · · · · · xix

Chapter 1: Dissecting The Novel · · · · · · · · · · · · · · · · · 1
    Six Ways Of Looking At A Novel · · · · · · · · · 4
    Spectacle · 6
    The Music Of Good Prose · · · · · · · · · · · · · 7
    Theme Or Meaning · · · · · · · · · · · · · · · · · · 11
    Character · 12
    The Supremacy Of Plot · · · · · · · · · · · · · · · 18
    Brainstormer #1 · 22

Chapter 2: What Is This Thing Called Plot? · · · · · · · · · · 24
    Movement Through Time · · · · · · · · · · · · · 26
    The Causal Chain · · · · · · · · · · · · · · · · · · · 29
    Increasing Intensity · · · · · · · · · · · · · · · · · · 34
    Rising Action · 35
    Plot And Story · 40
    Brainstormer #2 · 42

Chapter 3: The Plot Outline · 43
    The Apprentice's Toolbox · · · · · · · · · · · · · · 44
    The Process Of Outlining · · · · · · · · · · · · · · 46
    Creating The Chain Of Events · · · · · · · · · · 48
    Seeing Problems · 50
    Coincidence · 54
    Credibility · 55

    Appropriate Coincidences · · · · · · · · · · · · · · 58
    Brainstormer #3 · 59

Chapter 4: From Plot To Story · · · · · · · · · · · 61
    Making Connections · · · · · · · · · · · · · · · · · 61
    The Flashback · 64
    The Flash Forward · · · · · · · · · · · · · · · · · · 67
    Frame Stories · 69
    Outlining Your Story · · · · · · · · · · · · · · · · · 73
    Warning! Simple Is Good · · · · · · · · · · · · · · 76
    Brainstormer #4 · 77

Chapter 5: The Beginning · · · · · · · · · · · · · · 79
    The Reversal Of Fortune · · · · · · · · · · · · · · 81
    Starting With The Problem · · · · · · · · · · · · · 83
    The Set-Up · 88
    Revealing Backstory · · · · · · · · · · · · · · · · · 93
    Brainstormer #5 · 97

Chapter 6: Increasing Intensity · · · · · · · · · · 98
    Scenes And Chapters · · · · · · · · · · · · · · · · 99
    Cliffhanging · 100
    An Example · 101
    Cliffhanging Variations · · · · · · · · · · · · · · · 104
    The Tag Line · 107
    Leitmotifs · 110
    The Pause That Refreshes · · · · · · · · · · · · 114
    Another Mood Shift · · · · · · · · · · · · · · · · · 117
    Brainstormer #6 · · · · · · · · · · · · · · · · · · · 119
    Brainstormer #7 · · · · · · · · · · · · · · · · · · · 123

Chapter 7: The Ending · · · · · · · · · · · · · · · · 124
    Ambiguous Endings · · · · · · · · · · · · · · · · · 125
    The God Out Of The Machine · · · · · · · · · · 127

Expectations For The Ending · · · · · · · · · · · · · · · · · · · 129
Brainstormer #8 · 131

Chapter 8: Multiple Plots · 133
Parallel Plots · 133
Point Of View · 136
The Subplot · 138
Subplotting For Its Own Sake · · · · · · · · · · · · · · · · · · · 141
The 200-Pound Subplot · 142
Episodic Plotting · 145
Brainstormer #9 · 149

Chapter 9: Integrating Character And Plot · · · · · · · · · · · · · 151
Deeds, Not Words · 155
Choices · 158
Adjusting Character To Suit The Plot · · · · · · · · · · · · · 161
Adjust Plot To Reflect Character · · · · · · · · · · · · · · · · 163
The Patch · 164
Brainstormer #10 · 166

Chapter 10: Plots Ready-Made · 168
The Simplest Formula · 171
Another Way Of Looking At Formula Plotting · · · · · · · 173
Using Pre-Existing Plots · 174
Brainstormer #11 · 176
Brainstormer #12 · 177

Final Thoughts · 179

Introduction
Becoming A Better Writer

Like most writers—like most of you, I suspect—I started young, writing for sheer fun. Writing was play. You found a nice corner in a school library or in the back of a walk-in closet, then you curled up with a lined spiral notebook and retreated into yourself. You can never lose the pleasure of those times. You fabricated adventures. You imagined dangers. You created perfect worlds with imaginary beasts or evil worlds with heroes who conquered those evils. Princes from another planet might rescue a scullery maid from drudgery and lead her to become a princess. A tyrannosaurus rex named "Scaly" could be the pet and protector of a girls' club that meets after middle school in a hidden cave in Central Park in New York City. Anything could happen! Ideas tumbled out like fruits and vegetables and tin cans falling out of a grocery bag dropped on an apartment staircase, rolling and landing who knows where. Breathlessly, you filled pages until you were exhausted, living these stories in your head as you created them, never minding that it was all for fun. You delighted in the sheer pleasures of creation.

At some point, of course, most of us showed our writings to someone else, maybe mom or dad, sure that the stories that moved us so much would also move them. The usual outcome would be polite, if condescending. Most of our readers were not writers and had no idea how to give meaningful advice. If they did, we were not mature enough to receive and digest it. The whole situation invited "kind words": "Yeah, I like that. Real good. Did you walk the dog?"

You didn't have to be very perceptive to figure out that you were being shooed away, that your chosen critics were underwhelmed, but also didn't want to say your story wasn't very impressive.

"You didn't like it?" you'd follow up.

"No, it's good. Didn't I say it was good?"

The impatient tone told you your reader was irritated at being pressed. You'd begin to recognize (from your own reading and from seeing the flaws in your own storytelling) that there was more to writing than simply imagining cool things.

That "more" you might find after years and years, pages and pages, of trial and error. Many great writers had little formal training in writing, which is why many people fantasize that writers are born with a fully-armed with an array of talents and skills. Yet, when we look into their histories we usually find years of practice and failure. Some are lucky enough to fall into a relationship with a mentor whose advice more quickly improves whatever basic talents the learning writer has. Ernest Hemingway famously said he learned how to write by trying to please his editors as a reporter at the Kansas City Star and later at the Toronto Star. Mark Twain, Nina George, and Geraldine Brooks are also among the many novelists who learned to write better as journalists. Hemingway furthermore came under the guidance of Gertrude Stein in Paris, although her writing is very different from his. In more recent times, many would-be writers sign up for courses at a local college or enroll for creative writing degrees at universities like Iowa, Virginia, Southern California, Johns Hopkins University, New York University, and many others, large and small. These programs, if you can afford them, give you much time for developing your skills, provide guidance from professionals, and acquaint you with people who, like you, share the compulsion to write.

And, after all, what are you really looking for when you do these things? You are searching for "the secret." You want to know what it is that Stephen King knows, or Danielle Steele, or Margaret Atwood, or Colson Whitehead, or John Grisham. Something makes them successful, makes publishers fight over their books, makes readers order their books in advance. After all, you work hard on making your writing better. You have twists in your stories and characters as interesting as many in bestseller books? How come these people are artistic and monetary successes while you are still fighting the morning rush hour? They must know something you don't, right? Frustrated writers often get hung up on things like margins, word counts, fonts, and research. Others desperately try to figure out what is "hot," only to find out that "hot" has already cooled. There seem to be a lot of space alien serial killer romances on the bestseller list—maybe I need to write one of those!

What is hard to get your head around, however, is the fact that there is only one absolute rule in writing: *all that matters is whether or not the story is interesting.*

The difficulty comes when you try to define "interesting." You know it when you see it, but how do you make it happen for you? Fortunately, whatever secrets there are have been known for thousands of years, probably since some Neanderthal told his family how, against all odds, he brought down the king mastodon. There are no secrets to writing any more than there are secrets about how to throw a baseball or how to sauté a chicken breast. Obviously, some pitchers and cooks are better than others, but there aren't any real secrets. There are techniques you can learn and objectives you can seek as you perfect your techniques, but there is nothing hidden from you if you seek it out.

This book won't find comrades or a mentor for you, give you a degree to hang on your wall, or make time for you to write. These are up to you. What it can do, however, is give you an acquaintance with the most fundamental aspect of effective storytelling: plotting. On its most basic level, plotting is simple, but like many simple things, it can quickly become complex. Like Euclid's geometry, you start with points and lines, but these quickly spin up into the Pythagorean theorem and three-dimensional dodecahedrons. The points and lines on which powerful fiction is built is the plot.

Mastering Plot

Even the best plot can not be interesting if it is dragged down by unbelievable characters, poor phrasing, a herd of clichés, nauseating sentiment, or appalling spelling and grammar. (The latter is becoming all common, you'll have noticed.) There are so many judgments, so many choices to be made in writing. Do I break the chapter here? Will my reader be turned off by this violence? Do I use this word instead of that? Do I have my main character eat monkey brains or peppering pears?

And yet, the most brilliant characters and scenes you can imagine will all be wasted if the plot fails.

This book examines how plots have been used over the centuries and into the present by successful writers. I hope to offer you more ideas and greater understanding into how to approach the problems of plotting. There is nothing new under the sun, wrote Ecclesiastes, and you can bet that whatever problems you're facing with plotting have been faced by millions of writers over the centuries. You'll feel Sophocles and Chaucer and Jane Austen are all looking over your shoulder, but don't let them intimidate you. They sympathize. Yes, you're writing a novel and the novel has only been around for a few hundred years, but plotting is the basic foundation of all storytelling.

Plot is so fundamental that it shows up in any number of ways. A plot might find form as an oral epic poem, as a play, as a motion picture, or as your very own best-selling novel. That's why you will find in the following pages that I use examples of plot technique from many media and genres. A novelist can learn a lot about plotting from William Shakespeare, Francis Ford Coppola, and Homer, though none of them ever wrote a novel.

This book also tries to help you to understand why plot and various techniques of plotting work. If good writing shows itself in many forms, then you must be able to judge for yourself when your writing is succeeding. The only way to know whether you are succeeding is to know your purpose. You need a set of aesthetic values, touchstones that help you gauge whether you are succeeding. Therefore, the question of *why* certain things happen in the plots of our best novels, motion pictures, plays, etc. is crucial. It sometimes takes a lot of scratching to see what's underneath the distractingly bright paint of a fresh, new novel, but scratch we must!

If writing is a way of life, thinking like a writer is part of that life. At various points in the book, I offer what I call "Brainstormers." These are exercises designed to get you to look at plotting as a writer should. They will loosen up the sludge in the creative pipes and get the ideas flowing again. Many beginning writers have plenty to say. They have deep feelings, profound thoughts, a sure sense of people and setting, but they run into problems on the story structure level. Remember that the word "fiction" comes from the Latin word for "making." Writing involves craft, the act of "making."

Most readers react directly and do not consider the making of the novel. They only know that a novel is boring, disappointing, repetitive, brilliant, shocking, or surprising. They are like the man who buys a painting because it matches the sofa, or because it has King Charles spaniels in it. He gives little thought as to how the painting was composed, or how the painter blended the edge of one color area into another. He does not see the creativity in the craft, because he doesn't think about craft.

But you are the maker of your novel. You have to think about techniques and structures. You must read books differently than readers do. You must write considering things that only other writers will consider. I've published eight novels so far, been nominated for several awards, and feel daunted every time I begin to write. I think any writer worth a hoot feels this way, and writers who don't feel they could improve are universally dreadful. Scared writers are usually better writers.

The beginning writer is little different from the accomplished writer in this: both experienced and inexperienced writers imagine a novel with its characters, setting, plot diction, tone and all of its elements working in perfect harmony. But when we have written it we can always imagine it being better. When we write we are seeking to create an ideal novel, a Platonic novel which can never exist in the real world. All writers, are, after all, imaginers. Regardless how skilled we become, we can always imagine a higher level of writing. Chess genius José Raoul Capablanca once made the mistake of bragging that he had "mastered the game." He promptly lost the world championship and never regained it. Writers who think they are masters are just as finished. We strive for perfection, even though we know that it is impossible to attain, and if we do it seriously enough, we *do* get better.

Your choosing to read this book indicates that you wish to develop or refine your ability to use plot. Maybe you have great verbal skill. Maybe you are filled with great ideas or passions you want to share with the world. Plotting, however, seems a bit mysterious to you. How do you get your idea to behave like a story over the course of three hundred pages? This means, whether you are a beginner or an accomplished writer, that you are far from finished in your quest to be a better writer. Your working to be better *will* make you better. It may be a slow process, but your work will be rewarded.

A novel is a great adventure. It is an adventure of mind and feeling. The writing of one requires all your skills and sensitivities. Time and space are no hindrance to you. You can become a woman in love, a miner on Titan, or a flea crawling between the ears of a dog. You can make onions talk and carpets listen. You can create a just world or a village of no pity. Not everybody wants to do this sort of thing, but, admit it, you do. You wouldn't have picked up this book if you didn't. Sure learning to write a novel is a lot of work! But the work is worth it, and you are one of those special people who know it.

Enough of that. Let's get started.

—J. Madison Davis

Chapter 1
Dissecting The Novel

Reading for the plot, we learned somewhere in the course of our schooling, is a low form of activity.
—Peter Brooks

You need to know about people far more than you need to know about mechanical plot devices.
—Rita Mae Brown

I am led therefore to suppose that a good plot—which, to my own feeling, is the most insignificant part of a tale,—is that which will most raise it or most condemn it in popular judgement.
—Anthony Trollope

Surely it was time someone invented a new plot, or that the author came out from the bushes.
—Virginia Woolf

I don't work with plots ... Plot implies narrative and a lot of crap.
—John Cheever

Generally I don't even have a plot.
—Norman Mailer

Mastering Plot

I never make notes; just a few small details when I'm writing, but nothing much. The plot is never written down
—Ruth Rendell

I think books with weak or translucent plots can survive if the character being drawn along the path is rich, interesting and multi-faceted. The opposite is not true.
—Michael Connelly

Conspiracy! Intrigue! A rapidly thickening plot! Add some bestiality and a lecherous priest and I'd say you have the beginnings of a beautiful novel
—Marquis de Sade

I don't have a name and I don't have a plot. I have the typewriter and I have white paper and I have me, and that should add up to a novel.
—William Saroyan

Real life seems to have no plots.
—Ivy Compton-Burnett

You don't need convoluted plot lines. You don't need long-lost brothers.
—Ricky Gervais

If you move your characters from plot point to plot point, like painting by the numbers, they often remain stick figures
—Richard North Patterson

I don't plot my books rigidly, follow a preconceived structure. A novel mustn't be a closed system –it's a quest
—Kurt Vonnegut

I'm really quite bad at coming up with plot ideas. I like to create characters and just see what will happen to them when I let them loose!
—Judy Blume

How did "plot" get to be such a four-letter word?

If you read interviews with many prominent authors, like those preceding this chapter, you will notice how many of them seem to turn up their noses at the mention of plot. "I never begin with plot," they'll say. "Character [or situation or setting or thought] is where I begin my novels."

What's the implication? Only *bad* authors begin with plot. Some of these writers don't just imply it, they say it: a well-plotted book just isn't really "artistic." Books like that are for the great mass of dunderheads who read trash, not for us sophisticates who appreciate literature.

And how often have you heard or read the word "plot-driven" used in a negative sense? The most insignificant reviewers in the smallest local papers all seem to know it, along with anyone who presumes to have the last word on judging literature.

"Although Pylon De Violin's weepy novel is plot-driven, it nonetheless has a few good qualities," writes the reviewer.

"The thing I hate about Ty Wunnon's bestsellers is that they're all plot-driven," sniffs the socialite swirling her cocktail.

"Romances are like westerns and other popular literature," announces the professor, pausing to light his pipe, "*plot-driven*." (And, therefore, beneath contempt.)

When people condemn plot, they are often claiming for themselves some high Parnassian ground. To them, plot is the least thing for an author to consider. Literary artists give no thought to plot. That is something only "hacks" worry about. Plot is one of those regrettable things that only inferior readers enjoy. To this way of thinking, the enthusiast who says "I like a book with a good plot!" might as well be saying, "Yessirree, what I wouldn't give for roast possum like maw usedta make!"

In casual conversations the use of the word "plot" is often rather imprecise, as if people were not clear on what a plot is. For some of them, the plot seems to be surprises in the story line. "That book has a great plot! I didn't know what would happen next!" Others seem to think a plot is just what happens: "The plot is silly. A woman loses her husband to the maid."

Plot, however, is more than just a series of events or surprises. If we think of the plot as the frame of a building, and that building is a novel, we can understand that the girders, foundation pillars, beams, and joists of a building are not what we see when the building is finished. The brick veneer, the slate shingles, the way the window wraps the kitchen sink, and the sweep of the staircase are all things we might absorb and delight in as we look at a new house.

The fact that the structure of the house is strictly regulated by building codes so that it won't fall down, seems uncreative. The frame of a house might be beautiful to someone who appreciates frames, but isn't much more than a curiosity to most people. Studs in most walls are regulated as to their size and distance apart. The weight of each floor must be carefully calculated, as well as the location of load-bearing walls. Cost determines some aspects of framing, too. It is cheaper to put plumbing within a wall which has, say, a bathroom and a laundry room on opposite sides. All of these things relating to the structure of the house can seem dull and uncreative, though any architect will tell you they are not.

What's most important about all this, of course, is that if the structural work is badly done, the house may sag, lean to one side, even fall down. When the brick veneer starts popping off, the doors go trapezoidal, and the floor slopes, no house seems lovely.

Similarly, a novel with a bad structure may have many fine aspects, but ultimately parts of it sag, there are gaps, and the reader becomes annoyed and ultimately bored.

The ultimate crime in writing is to be boring. You risk that every time you are careless with your plot.

SIX WAYS OF LOOKING AT A NOVEL

People have been telling stories since most human beings gave up grunting for speech, and writing a novel is participating in this ancient tradition. Although technology may change how we communicate stories, human nature hasn't changed and there are many principles of storytelling that remain as true as when some Minoan entertained his family by the hearth.

I mentioned earlier in this book that the "secrets" of storytelling were known almost from the beginning. Perhaps the earliest commentator to warn writers about the importance of plot in storytelling was Aristotle (384-322 B.C.), one of the greatest minds of his—and any other—time. He wrote on subjects as varied as political theory, morality, natural science, physics, and rhetoric. He also applied his genius to the theater and wrote a book, *The Poetics*, about the history and form of drama.

Although the part of the book explaining comedy has been lost for centuries, the surviving portion of this essay is as alive as when it was written. It has influenced the art of storytelling even among writers who have never actually read *The Poetics*. Most "how-to" books are second or third-hand updates of *The Poetics*, expanding, but not really improving, Aristotle's insights.

What has *The Poetics* to do with the novel? The novel didn't become popular in Europe until eighteen hundred years after Aristotle died! As it turns out, however, reading *The Poetics* is one of the most valuable things any novelist, dramatist, or screenwriter can do.

While there are obvious differences among media such as novels, dramas, and motion pictures, they are all forms of storytelling. The structure of storytelling has consistency, even if the method of storytelling does not. Novels must be as "dramatic" as drama, or they are a dull read. An effective plot may become a great novel, play, or movie. Much of Aristotle's dissection of drama also applies to the novel.

Aristotle tells us that there are six basic elements to the drama: plot, character, diction, thought, spectacle, and lyric poetry (this is often translated as "music"). There is nothing sacred about these six; however, they are handy as a way of analyzing the elements of a novel, and demonstrating the importance of plot. We must always remember, however, that none of the elements stands alone. To use our metaphor of architecture again, a house consists of rooms and walls, but a wall is not a house. A plot without specific characters is not a novel; characters or spectacle without a plot cannot make a novel.

SPECTACLE

Let's begin with what Aristotle calls the least important element of drama, spectacle, and build up to what he considers most important, plot. In drama, spectacle includes such things as costumes, scenery, and stage effects—the elements created for a particular stage performance. Even the actor's facial expressions could be said to be part of the spectacle.

All of these things can be an enormous part of the pleasure of a live performance. Everyone who sees the helicopter land on stage in *Miss Saigon*, or the parade of elephants and cheetahs in Giuseppe Verdi's opera *Aida*, remembers these moments with delight. In movies, too, spectacle is a major part of the pleasure. The recent vogue in superhero movies depends heavily on spectacle. What would these movies be like without explosions, bodily metamorphoses, and death rays?

How does spectacle apply to the novel? Since a novel takes place on paper and in the head of the reader, it is hard to make a direct equivalent to spectacle, but you might consider it to be the sensationalism of a book. In Tolstoy's *War and Peace*, the battle of Borodino is described in great detail and is breathtaking for its grandeur. In the context of that great novel this spectacle is certainly appropriate and adds to the pleasure. My grandmother often spoke of Liza's escape across the river ice in *Uncle Tom's Cabin* by Harriet Beecher Stowe. She had read the novel serialized in a newspaper in the 1920s. The spectacle of that episode was vivid in her mind until she died in the 1970s.

On the negative side of spectacle, we have many books and movies that seem to think they can carry the story with unconvincing characters and absurdly gory descriptions, or CGI splendors and room-shaking sounds. Almost anything goes, but that doesn't make the experience rewarding. Some years ago (1981) there was a low-budget movie called *Scanners*. The opening consisted of a sequence in which a man's head exploded. The audience up to that time had never seen anything like that, and today, this is basically all the film is famous for. The clip is readily available on You Tube, but what the rest of the movie is about is quickly forgotten. Aficionados of director David Cronenberg find it interesting as an example of Cronenberg's early work, but Cronenberg conceded that the movie was written on the fly, as it was being shot. Rather than a full, cohesive story, *Scanners* had one amazing spectacle, the exploding head. In the sequel to *The Silence of the Lambs*, Thomas Harris's *Hannibal*, we have such spectacular scenes as a character having his feet eaten off by pigs, and Hannibal Lector slicing and sauteeing the brain of a living man to feed it to Starling. Some readers, I suppose, found pleasure in it, but most thought *Silence of the Lambs* was a far more memorable book.

Sex scenes are often part of contemporary novels and might be considered spectacle, also. They usually do little to advance the plot, revealing nothing much about the characters, and may be included merely for their shock value or titillation—if shock value and titillation are even possible any more. A lengthy description of a sex act may provide pleasure to the reader, but it usually advances the story no more than the sentence "They made love until dawn."

As with the other five elements in Aristotle's analysis of a story, the value of spectacle depends on how well it is done. There is nothing inherently wrong with spectacle. It shouldn't be neglected as a source of pleasure for your reader. Yet, it is easy to agree with what Aristotle observes, that it is the least important element in a drama, and by extension, one of the least important in creating an effective novel. One spectacular scene after another does not make a novel. They must be connected.

To use the house metaphor again, a jumble of expensive rolls of wallpaper, gargoyles, and stacked bricks do not make a mansion.

THE MUSIC OF GOOD PROSE
The fifth most important element of drama, Aristotle tells us, is lyric poetry or music. A lot of chanting or singing by the chorus was part

of ancient drama, and musicians played a large part. It was similar to what we see in modern musicals. Fantine is fired from her job in the musical *Les Miserables* and contemplates her life by singing "I Dreamed a Dream." Henry Higgins gets exasperated by Eliza's behavior in *My Fair Lady* and sings "Why Can't a Woman Be More Like a Man?"

In motion pictures, the musical score influences our emotions greatly, though we often barely notice it. Bernard Herrmann's scores for *Psycho* and *Cape Fear* make us edgy. Hildur Guðnadóttir's score for *Joker* expresses the mood of that film perfectly, as does Thomas Newman's score for *1917*. How about John Williams's scores for *Star Wars*, *E.T.: the Extraterrestrial*, *Jaws*, *The Rise of Skywalker*, and *Saving Private Ryan*? These and many other composers made the films they scored twice as effective. On the other hand, bad scoring for a film is monstrously grating and can ruin the whole effect for us.

Recently a novel was published accompanied by a compact disc the reader was to listen to while reading. Barring such novelties, there is no direct correspondence between the music of a drama and what's in a novel. However, drama in ancient times was always poetic, used meter, and might be rhymed. Up until realism took over, poetic drama was the rule, not the exception. Certainly, there is a rhythm and power derived from the use of language in a novel.

Great writers manipulate the rhythms and sound of their "music." Edgar Allan Poe's prose feels like the creepiness he wishes us to feel. The lengthy, fluid sentences of William Faulkner, Marcel Proust, and Gabriel García-Márquez create a sense of time overlapping time, in which the past is always a part of the present. The short sentences of Ernest Hemingway or Dashiell Hammett convey a tight sense of immediacy. The patterns of wording in Jamaica Kincaid give a Caribbean sound to her prose. James Baldwin and Toni Morrison make us feel the rhythms and variety of African-American speech and culture. Willa Cather does the same with midwesterners.

A great part of the musical effect comes from what Aristotle calls diction, the "expression through choice of words." English is a particularly rich and subtle language to write in. Consider the following words:

> obese
> fat
> overweight
> corpulent
> abdominous
> beer-bellied
> heavyset
> queen-sized
> tub of lard
> gut-bucket
> elephantine
> chubby
> zaftig

All of these are ways of saying someone has more weight than is average. The words, however, vary in the degree of insult or "fat shaming" implied by them. "Overweight" is fairly neutral: it neither condemns nor praises. "Zaftig," "chubby," and "queen-sized" are more positive. "Obese" has health connotations. "Beer-bellied" implies a way of life, and has a comic quality. "Abdominous" has a comic sound that "corpulent" and "heavyset" lack. "Gut-bucket" is a cruder insult than "elephantine."

The *Oxford English Dictionary* lists about 616,500 words. The largest dictionaries of German (the second largest language in vocabulary) have only about 185,000 words. English speakers grow up learning many subtleties in our rich vocabulary, which grows richer by 5,000 words a year. People learning English find such differences a nightmare. If you say a man is "cool," you praise him. If you say he's "not so hot," it's an insult. The context makes so much difference.

Some words fit in some social contexts and not others. Some sex words are distasteful in certain contexts, but not in others, just as certain manners are required at a formal dinner, but seem odd at a barbeque. Other sex words are clinical and sound too medical to use in intimate settings, though newscasters will resort to them when they gleefully uncover the latest scandal.

How many euphemisms do we rely on? They, too, have their own contexts and a meaning quite different from the literal. For the sake of clarity in your writing, stylists say to avoid them, but sometimes euphemisms like "powder her nose" are more appropriate to the occasion. "Powder her nose" is also a sex-linked euphemism. Imagine a man using the phrase to refer to his own trip to "the little boys' room." The contexts invoke many unwritten rules.

Do you think the outlaw Jesse James ever used the words "zaftig" or "bonhomie"? Or that medieval peasants argued about the "oppression of the capitalist system" as they did in *Monty Python and the Holy Grail*? Using expressions out of context is a well-recognized way to create comedy.

The great French novelist Gustave Flaubert wrote to his girlfriend Louise Colet about his struggles to find *le mot juste*, the perfect word to fit the situation. He spent hours figuring out how to express things, because the expression has so much to do with the effect. Every writer who wants to do well can certainly understand that and sympathize with Flaubert's struggle. Been there! Done that! We all know how important it is. The wrong word may leave the wrong impression and turn your good guy into an insensitive clod. The right word will leave readers sighing, knowing that no other word describes this or that quite as well.

There is a pirated version of *Hamlet* called the "Bad Quarto" by scholars. The thieves got the jist of the play for publication, but not the exact words. In the version we know, Hamlet says, "To be or not to be: that is the question." In the Bad Quarto he says, "To be or not to be: aye, there's the rub." Funny, isn't it? As a child, I grew up in King James Bible country and knew "My cup runneth over" in the Twenty-third Psalm as properly reverent. When my brother and I first heard the translation which goes, "My cup overflows" we broke out in uproarious, irreverent laughter. As the bumper sticker I once saw said, "If it ain't King James, it ain't Bible." "Overflows" just wasn't Bible. Word choice is essential to the impact any piece of writing has, novels included.

Yet, the word choices and the rhythms of prose alone do not sustain any novel. They work in the service of more fundamental elements of a novel. Sometimes the most mundane and flattest prose we read may be interesting because of the information it contains. Even the dullest technical manual has a style. It may not be an interesting style, but it serves its purpose. The word choices and rhythms of prose can add greatly to how interesting a story is, but they cannot replace the more fundamental elements.

THEME OR MEANING

The third most important element of dramatic writing to Aristotle is thought. Immediately this brings to mind what is called "theme" in a novel, or the overall message or statement of the work. We hear books summed up in such statements as "The theme of *Moby Dick* is the inability of humanity to know God," or "The theme of Toni Morrison's *Beloved* is the cruel legacy of slavery." A closer reading of Aristotle reveals that he probably has in mind something much less general. He seems to mean the argument or process of thought in the dialogue of his characters. Thus, his "thought" might be the mentality of the characters, or what we call their intellectual motivations, or even the form of their rhetoric.

But we are not here to argue the subtleties of translating ancient Greek. We can certainly agree that whatever Aristotle means precisely, it is not the most important element in a drama or a novel. No one enjoys a great play simply because it has a great message. Otherwise the greatest plays in English literature would be the medieval morality plays, like *Everyman*. Shakespeare's message is often contradictory or ambiguous, even though his plays are filled with moral content. If messages were the most important things in motion pictures, then propaganda films as a group would be more compelling than dramatic films.

The same applies to novels. Why bother with a story when the moral is all that matters? The story of George Washington and the cherry tree was a fiction concocted by a Parson Weems. Does anyone actually read the original story any more? Its moral is the most memorable aspect of it. What is the moral, on the other hand, of *Gone Girl*? Millions of people bought it and read it. Did they do it for the message? What was the message? Don't trust the person you marry?

No, to paraphrase Samuel Goldwyn, to send messages you should text or use Facebook. The writer who is writing well may have many interesting thematic concerns which will enrich a novel. However, the vitality of the novel resides in the down-to-earth details of who does what to whom, and how.

As with the beauty of language, a book can be very impressive in the power of its thought but it cannot be sustained by that alone. If you ask a novelist what she is writing about, she will say, "A guy who tries to rob Fort Knox." If you ask someone who isn't yet a novelist, he will say, "It's about the materialism of the American middle class." The latter person should be writing philosophy or something, but until he learns to love guys who plan to rob Fort Knox, he won't be a novelist.

CHARACTER

Aristotle astonishes people by stating that character is less important than plot. And we need to spend some time examining this issue because 1) so many writers state absolutely that character is most important and 2) I agree with Aristotle. Our particular interest in guys who plan to rob Fort Knox, women who borrow lawn mowers, football players who contract diseases, teenagers who sell shoes in the summer, and Danish princes who fall in love would seem to indicate that character is the heart and soul of a story, whether it is a play, movie, or novel. So many ideas for stories come from meeting interesting people.

Yet, often what is interesting about people we meet or read about is the story of what they have done or undergone. Is the character of serial killer Ed Gein interesting? He was the real person who inspired both the authors of *Psycho, The Silence of the Lambs,* and hundreds of other novels. Why is the character of Ed Gein interesting? Because he did horrible, inconceivable things. We'd like to know what could make a person do things like that. We'd like to know what his character was, what was inside him. Yet, how do we know what was inside him? Because of what he did.

Are we engaging in a chicken and egg argument here? Which came first: the internal qualities (his character) or what he did (his acts)? In a story, what is more important, the motivations or the acts?

As I wrote earlier, the elements of a novel cannot be separated to stand alone. A brick and a plank are not a house, but put enough of them together properly and you'll have a house. It helps, however, to remember that Aristotle is writing about drama. In a play, what means do we have to know the internal aspects of a character? We find out who they are by what they say and do. We find out Othello's weakness because he falls for Iago's scheme to make him jealous of Desdemona. We find out the profound depth of his weakness and the ferocity of his temper because he strangles the innocent woman. We find out that Beatrice is clever in *Much Ado About Nothing* because she verbally spars with Benedict. We find out how much Romeo loves Juliet because he kills himself over her.

Consider one of the stories in the Bible. Abraham has finally in his old age fathered a son by his wife Sarah. Because of the long struggle to create an heir, we can imagine easily that the boy Isaac is the most precious thing in his life. God, however, demands that Abraham sacrifice Isaac. What a cruel demand! What will Abraham do? He takes his son to the chosen place. He puts the boy on a sacrificial altar. He raises the knife and is about to strike when an angel stays his hand. God was testing Abraham to find out if he, above all of his deepest feelings, is obedient to God's commands. Abraham demonstrates he is. His descendants will become the chosen people.

Abraham has been placed under terrible stress. Few men in his situation could find it in themselves to obey their gods in this way. Abraham's character is defined by his act. However we regard him for this, we know he's made of steel. We couldn't know what he was made of if he didn't do these things.

On the surface it looks like God needed some proof of Abraham's inner strength, but the character of God in this story has been interpreted many ways. God knows he isn't going to allow Abraham to kill Isaac, doesn't he? Or does he change his mind at the last minute? Wouldn't God know that Abraham will act as he does? If so, does this test really consist of demonstrating to Isaac and to Abraham himself, Abraham's inner strength?

I'm not trying to start a theological discussion here, but I am trying to show how a simple plot and the events in it, bring out the interior qualities and potentials we call character. The Bible and many other works often deal with character by simply saying something like, "In the city of Sodom dwelt a good man named Lot," or "Ruth was a pious woman." But such remarks are always followed by demonstrations in plot of the blanket statements. In stories we know characters from *what they do.*

Sometimes characters in plays speak what are supposed to be their innermost thoughts (the soliloquy), and in motion pictures we may hear the thoughts of a character while seeing something else (the voice-over). Mostly, however, we access characters' minds when they speak to others. There are often characters in plays and movies who seem to be there mostly to be the confidant who allows the main character to speak freely. "Honey, I don't know what's gotten into you!" says the husband. The wife answers, "I can't get my father's death out of my mind. It keeps me awake." Her admission to her husband reveals her innermost thoughts. In the dramatic forms, we really don't know anything about the character until he or she does or says something.

In fiction, we may go more directly into a person's mind without using a convention to do so. In much fiction the words, "she thought" or "he thought" may be left out, and yet we still know that we are reading the character's thoughts. The technique of stream-of-consciousness, which was most famously used in a small section of James Joyce's

Ulysses and in William Faulkner's *The Sound and the Fury*, was supposed to simulate the scattered thought processes. After all, no one thinks in well-crafted grammatical sentences. However, stream of consciousness has never become a popular form of revealing inner thoughts. It is a convention which was more convincing when it was new, nearly a century ago, than it is now.

However we depict the mental processes we will be using a convention. And, in any case, if Aristotle were with us here, he might say, "Well, phooey, thinking is an act, too." If we can read what the character is thinking, the character is doing something. We fill in the nature of the person by the nature of his acts. Fiction may represent the thinking processes as well as they represent physical action. But is there any essential difference? A man kicks a dog in a way that implies he hates dogs. A man says he despises dogs. A man imagines slowly roasting the same dog in a fire. All these are overt acts that imply who this disturbed man is.

So what is character, after all? It is a set of inherent qualities in the imitation of a human being. What we call a character in a novel, play, or movie bears close resemblance to a human being, but is not one. People are far more complicated than characters. People are far less predictable than characters. Characters are designed to seem complicated and to act in some surprising ways, but they are actually more consistent. The behavior that seems surprising from characters is based upon a clear conception of their identity. In the simplest sort of story, for example, there are good guys and bad guys. The conception of their identities is very simple and their behavior is predicted by what the author values as good or bad.

As stories get more sophisticated, the lines between good and bad become fuzzier. A basically good character may be attracted to evil and even commit a bad act which he or she later regrets. A bad character might be attractive, witty, and love his mother. The point is, in the behavior of a character there is always some rationale behind it. Charles Foster Kane in *Citizen Kane* is motivated by the seizure of his sled when he was a child. We see the taking of the sled early in the film, but don't know exactly what it means. Emma Bovary in *Madame Bovary* is motivated by a desire to be someone special, a romantic heroine. The clues are given early in the novel when Flaubert describes her convent education and her interest in the romantic novels of French author Chateaubriand. This is not to say that either of these memorable characters is uncomplicated. They are complex, and interesting because they are complex. Yet they are not people. Compared to the dullest person in existence, Thomas Hardy supposedly said, the richest character in a novel is a mere bag of bones.

People's motivations are very confusing and usually dimly understood. The newspapers are full of terrible stories about kids who grow up in brutal households. One kid grows up to become a killer; another grows up to become a tireless charity worker. On the spur of the moment, one person commits an act of immeasurable courage while another holds back. Who can explain it? Richard Nixon grew up in economic difficulty. Hubert Humphrey grew up in similar circumstances. In 1968 they ran against each other for the presidency. Humphrey was a champion of minorities and the poor. Nixon's constituency was much more the upper and middle classes. We might speculate on the causes of their different attitudes, but we can never be sure.

An excess of a certain chemical in the bloodstream or a slight rearrangement of his genes might make a man more inclined to anger easily and commit violence. A little of another might turn him into a babbling idiot. Severe post-partum depression has made some women kill their babies. Sudden religious insights make some give away their material possessions and take to the road. We know such things happen and that they are often out of the control of the individual. Our science is not good enough to predict what a given individual's reaction may be to a particular stimulus, though it is often fairly obvious. Praise will usually make people happy and criticism will usually make them angry or sad.

Many people's reactions are so obvious that they are boring and that is another reason that story people are not like you and I. Even the most free-spirited of us has habits. We like to relax in certain ways, are irritated by certain habits, are offended by certain words, or turn to a particular beverage to calm down, whether it is warm milk or Jamaican rum. We awake at a certain time, read the paper, eat cereal, and leave for work at about the same time. That isn't very interesting, but the author needs to balance an illusion of consistency that resembles this reality against an illusion of unpredictability that resembles the capricious nature of real people.

Character, then, is all about the inner qualities of a story person and how these qualities determine the choices this person would make in a given situation. Parson Weems' George Washington had the quality of being scrupulously honest as a boy. Confronted with the question of who chopped down the cherry tree, he answers truthfully. Shakespeare's Richard III is evil, but courageous. Faced with an army larger than his own, he decides nonetheless to fight and is killed as a result. Scarlett O'Hara of *Gone With the Wind* is resilient and resourceful under the superficial behavior she presents to the world. When the worst possible things happen to her, she is never fully beaten. Even when Rhett leaves her, she picks herself up.

Those examples, and dozens of others, should tell us that we cannot know a character without that character undergoing a test. The test a character undergoes is the plot. That isn't all a plot is, but here we're just trying to see how these elements of a novel relate to one another.

In Mark Twain's *Extract from Captain Stormfield's Visit to Heaven*, Stormfield encounters Absalom Jones, a bricklayer from somewhere back of Boston. If he'd ever had the chance he would have been a greater general than Caesar, Hannibal, Alexander, and Napoleon. But he never had the chance because he had lost his thumbs and a few teeth. No recruiting surgeon would pass him. Stormfield also sees a tailor from Tennessee named Billings who "wrote poetry that Homer and Shakespeare couldn't begin to come up with." But nobody printed it, and all his ignorant neighbors laughed at it. In the heaven that Stormfield visits these injustices are remedied, but on earth, they remain injustices. These men's chances to prove themselves a general and a poet never materialized. The plot of a story is the war that creates a general and the publication that creates a poet. Without the struggle of a plot, those potential qualities remain potential and the character is a cipher.

THE SUPREMACY OF PLOT

So, then, following this line of reason takes us back to Aristotle's statement that plot is the most important element of a drama and mine, that it is *the* essential element in a novel. Good plotting will not necessarily make a novel good. Weak thought, poor word choices, characters who seem inconsistent, and spectacle at the expense of common sense can easily make a novel laughable, regardless of the plot. However, without a plot, a novel is a disorganized meander.

Many great writers have used worn-out plots and revitalized them. The story of Faust selling his soul to the devil is one example. It first showed up in Germany during the fifteenth century in something called the *Faustbuch*. Christopher Marlowe wrote a great play based on it. Johann Wolfgang von Goethe wrote a long poem that is one of the masterpieces of German literature. Charles Gounod and Arrigo Boito both wrote great operas based on it. Thomas Mann used it to create a powerful novel. Clive Barker's *The Damnation Game* and Terry Pratchett's *Eric* are Faustian stories.

There are many in the history of literature, opera, and theater. These Fausts are different in many aspects of their characterization, language, thought, and spectacle, but the underlying plot is—if not the same—very similar. Undoubtedly many terrible writings, fortunately forgotten, also use the Faust plot. There are so many ways a writer can ruin a book with a good plot that perhaps this is one reason why so many writers have said that plot isn't very important. A book with a good plot can turn out to be a work of absolute genius or a dung heap of nonsense. Why in the world would we want to regard the plot as the primary element?

If we wish to become successful novelists, we must ask ourselves what it is that keeps readers reading. Few people would disagree with the remark that readers get interested in a situation and want to know what happens next. Let's imagine that you're walking down a hallway one day and you turn a corner and encounter this situation. A couple is shouting at each other. The woman is weeping; the man is red-faced and gesturing wildly.

Do you walk on as if the hall were empty? Do you ignore it? Of course not. You want to know what's going on. You walk a little more slowly, all ears. It wouldn't be polite to butt in, but if you happen to know someone in a nearby office, you might ask them what all that is about. If you happen to be going into a nearby office, you may try to eavesdrop (Go on! Yes, you would.) You will take a peek now and then just to see the argument doesn't get out of hand. Your mind will run through possibilities.

Each word you pick up will turn into a clue for the story you're constructing in your mind. They're married. They're not married. Did she say "blood test"? She has an incurable disease. She's pregnant. He's tested positive for drugs—*again*. She's discovered that their son's DNA doesn't match theirs, or doesn't match his. His cholesterol is sky-high, which means he hasn't been taking his medication.

Most people could come up with a dozen simple explanations without much effort. If you're a creative person, you could spin this out for days and come up with explanations from the sublime to the ridiculous to the bizarre. How about she just discovered that her husband has the blood of an extraterrestrial?

On its simplest level, a story works on us this way. There is some sort of problem that has an uncertain outcome. Mentally, we get caught up in the problem as if it were our own and seek hypothetical solutions. Maybe the woman will leave him. Maybe he will slap her. Maybe she will pull out a knife and stab him. Maybe six thugs will come around the corner and beat them up. Or maybe an earthquake will interrupt their argument and they will come to know how much they love each other.

We can't help trying to fill in the blanks when we see an unusual situation. Who knows why this is. Presumably it has to do with primate evolution and the way our brains got wired. The important thing is that we do it. We want to know what happens next in a compelling situation, and we're willing to hang around to find out.

A story which lacks the quality of progression (the sense that more interesting things are coming) will convince very few people to hang around. The progression is the essence of story telling, and the plot is a road map of that progression.

If we make up a plot for our arguing couple it might go like this:

> Lulu Whiteprot grew up in a household which was otherwise loving, but highly bigoted. She met and married Charlie Siciliano, but it was quite a struggle to convince her family to accept a Catholic. They are polite to him, and things have settled down. During a routine blood test, Charlie discovers he has sickle-cell anemia. It is a very mild case, but implies to Lulu that Charlie has African-American ancestors. Now she knows her family will never accept Charlie and grandfather Nathan Forrest Whiteprot will write Lulu out of his will. Charlie tries to explain that some southern Europeans also show sickle-cells, probably from the Moorish invasions of the Middle Ages. He gets a doctor to explain this to her, but she cannot believe it, thinking the doctor is saying it for Charlie's sake. The marriage is doomed because she believes Charlie is a liar and if her family ever finds out she'll have no family. They separate after Charlie calls Lulu's family "a buncha morons." A week later, grandfather Whiteprot shocks the family by announcing he's been a fool all his life. He is in love with his African-American nurse at the retirement home and love is more important than race. Lulu rushes back to Charlie and he forgives her.

Now, this is not going to be the Great American novel, but it is a plot. The problem begins when the results of the blood test are known. They end when Lulu accepts the error of her ways. The progression of these events is a plotline.

Now let's just repeat the fact that this might seem like a silly plot, but that does not mean it couldn't be written brilliantly. It might be a major challenge, but comedy comes to mind. Shakespeare made a lot of great plays out of some pretty silly plots. So much depends upon how well and convincingly the characters are portrayed. So much depends on how wittily the dialog is written. So much depends upon the spectacle of each scene and setting.

But the plot is the frame of the novel. Without it, the novel will not stand.

If you still refuse to believe plot is the most fundamental element of a novel, I'd advise you to take a look at the market. Consider what *bad* books you have read. There is a great deal to be learned from bad books if you make an effort. Why were those books bad? Is it the language? The characterization? It should be obvious, if you think about it, that a poorly written book with a well-constructed plot is more likely to be published than a poorly written book with a weak plot.

The most popular best sellers and genre novels—mystery, suspense-thriller, horror, romance, western, fantasy, science-fiction, and even mainstream novels—are all built around plot. Most "literary" novels are plotted, also, whether their authors admit it or not. A plot doesn't have to be action oriented. It can be psychological and internal. Many authors might not begin with a plot in mind, but they usually end up with one in their books. Very rarely a well-written book with hardly any plot at all will get published as a "literary" work and even win awards. Does it ever become popular? Almost never. I can't think of an example. Even *Finnegans Wake* by James Joyce, the ultimate literary experiment, known as the most difficult book ever written, has a plot under all that language bending. It's elusive, but it is there.

Many a published novel lacks good characterization, powerful emotion, surprising situations, or good writing. Plot can carry a book if it's solid enough. Other aspects of the novel cannot come close without real genius behind them, and often, not then.

Mastering Plot

BRAINSTORMER #1

The purpose of this exercise is to get you to think about the way a novel is constructed, rather than just the overall effect.

Take one of your favorite novels, one that sticks in your mind as being one of the best you've ever read. You're not trying to impress anyone. Don't be snobbish and pick some certified, solid-gold classic, unless its one you really *enjoyed*.

Read it again, but as you read, note the appearances of each of the following elements: plot, character, theme or meaning, use of language (diction and "music"), and spectacle. These will overlap many times. A spectacular scene might also be one in which the use of language is particularly effective. You might make notes in the margins of your book, if it's a copy that isn't rare or expensive.

When you're finished, make five columns on a piece of paper, like this:

Plot	Character	Language	Theme	Spectacle

Think about each element separately and how important it is in making the novel good. Give it a percentage rating based on its relative importance. I would, for example, rate Charles Dickens' *A Christmas Carol* as follows.

Plot	Character	Language	Theme	Spectacle
20	30	7	23	20

The plot is very simple and moves well. The characters, as is often the case with Dickens, are unforgettable. Scrooge has become one of our most well-know characters. The language is okay—there are many famous lines—but it is often a bit tiresome. Of course the book has great effect because of the theme of human fellowship! That's why its such a big favorite at Christmas. The spectacle of the ghosts and Victorian London is also wonderful.

You might disagree with me on any of these. I might disagree with myself if I rethink this. However, it gets us thinking about how novels get made and how they are composed. You've got to think like a writer to be a writer.

Chapter 2
What Is This Thing Called Plot?

In the first chapter we discussed plot in a general way as an essential element in any story, whether it is a play, a film, or a novel. In this chapter I want to refine our terms so that we know exactly what we're discussing. However else other people understand—or misunderstand—the term "plot," this chapter will explain what *I* mean precisely by plot. Then, we'll be able to move on to the nitty gritty of how you can use that knowledge to construct effective plots. Better plotting is the first step to writing better novels.

The Greek word that scholars have translated as "plot" from Aristotle's *Poetics* is *mythos*, the word from which we get "mythology," "myth," and "mythic." If you look in several dictionaries of ancient Greek, as I did recently, you'll often find that they ignore Aristotle's narrower meaning and simply say that *mythos* means "story, fable, tale, or myth." This sense of the word is important. Without the plot, we have only characters, spectacle, and language—and no story.

We might also give some thought to myth itself and how ancient stories have survived for millennia, speaking vividly to new generations. The trials of Hercules, the hammer of Thor, the great flood which threatened Utnapishtim of the Sumerian story and Noah of the Hebrews: these and other myths resonate in the human heart far in time and space from their original sources. Something about these stories makes people respond to them in an emotional way that cannot be rationally explained. Whether, as Carl Gustav Jung theorized, they touch the common experiences of life and death that humans undergo, or, as Sigmund Freud said, they mirror our neuroses and help to resolve them, doesn't really matter. Myths recur in many forms and continue to work on the hearers or readers. A writer who can tap into the mysterious power of myth (and make it fresh) will revive these powerful subterranean emotions.

An example of this would be the Celtic myth of King Lear, which came up through several sources. It apparently originated in a myth about a river god. Shakespeare read and adapted the story for his play. In short, a king divides his kingdom among his daughters, mistaking the disloyal ones for the loyal one. He is ruined by it.

What is interesting about Shakespeare's great tragedy is that he, for some reason, understood the full implications of the story and changed the original myth's ending in which King Lear is restored to his throne and all is well. Shakespeare's king is brought to ruin and death. After the closing of the theaters because of the Puritan revolution, the play was rarely performed for a while and then was doctored to restore the happy ending. The tragedy was just too strong for the audiences.

The twentieth century, with World War I, the Holocaust, and the nuclear bomb allows us to understand the tragedy of Lear in a different way and we have no problem in seeing Shakespeare's wisdom. The logical outcome of the plot is tragic. Who among us hasn't made a mistake in loving someone who is a user? With Lear, it is even sadder because it is his daughters. The myth still resonates powerfully despite its obscure origin as a myth about a river god in Britain.

In 1992, Jane Smiley won a Pulitzer Prize with *A Thousand Acres*, a bestselling novel about a midwestern farmer based on King Lear. Akira Kurosawa, the great Japanese director, based his *Ran* (1985) upon *King Lear*, but changed the king's daughters into sons because it would have been almost impossible for daughters to rule a medieval Japanese kingdom. The details can be changed—names, time period, characterization—but underlying the story is a clear pattern.

So, then, we can say for a start, that a plot is an underlying pattern. It is a story ("myth," if you like), stripped of the details of language, spectacle, setting, and so forth, until only the structure is left. It is the conceptual framework of a story, but not the story itself. But what is the nature of this structure? How does each part of the structure relate to the other parts?

MOVEMENT THROUGH TIME

First, a plot moves chronologically. A plot begins at one point in time and progresses to a later time. A plot may cover a period of years or merely a few moments. A novel like Gabriel Garcia-Marquez's great work *One Hundred Years of Solitude*, covers generations of the Buendia family from its immigration to the village of Macondo until the last of the Buendias is carried away by jungle ants. Alex Haley's novel *Roots* also traces the history of a family. Many other novels concentrate on one central character's journey from cradle to grave, such as William Makepeace Thackeray's *Barry Lyndon*. Plotting a story over a long time period gives it an epic feel and it provides the pleasure we associate with the great old novels like *War and Peace* or *Silas Marner*. The reader enters what feels like a parallel universe and "lives" there for a while.

Lengthy plots such as these are more unusual in novels these days than they were in the past, due to the price of paper and other business considerations, but also because of the influence of the dramatic media, particularly the motion picture. Plays and motion pictures tend to concentrate on an intense period of conflict. Not as much can happen in a dramatization as happens in a short story or novel, simply because there isn't enough time. Nine hour movies are not the rule, but reading a novel for nine hours over a period of days wouldn't be unusual at all.

Not to mention the fact that showing usually takes more time than telling. "John grew up in a small town" *tells* what you need to know in a blink. *Showing* John's small town would take several shots in a motion picture. Remember that wonderful opening in the film *Forrest Gump*, in which the camera follows a feather blown past several scenes of a Georgia town? Setting up such a panorama of the small town our main character, John, grew up in would involve considerable expense for a film maker, not to mention figuring out what you *show* in a few seconds to illustrate the process of growing up in a small town. Even if a novelist takes a paragraph to describe the small town it won't take as much of the reader's time (as it would a viewer's) for the amount of information conveyed.

However, the amount of time a plot covers in fiction can also be very short. The most memorable example of this might be the brilliant short story by Ambrose Bierce, "An Occurrence at Owl Creek Bridge." Read it if you haven't. Spoiler alert! As you may recall, a Confederate spy is being hanged upon a bridge. As he drops, the rope breaks and he goes through an extraordinary, surreal escape back to his own plantation. Just as he is about to embrace his wife, the rope breaks his neck. He has imagined his entire escape as he dropped from his plank to the end of the rope. Bierce's ending is one of the greatest surprises in literature, yet is emotionally wrenching even when you know it is coming. As a whole, the plot takes place in seconds.

Novels have been done in the same way. A character goes over her entire life as the plane she is riding in develops mechanical trouble. A man fantasizes an entire lifetime with his bride in between the minister's question and his answer. In Mark Twain's *A Connecticut Yankee in King Arthur's Court* the adventures of the Yankee take place while he lies knocked out by a crowbar. *Alice in Wonderland* takes place during a dream which Alice has by a river. The huge 1969 bestseller, Irving Wallace's *The Seven Minutes*, concerned a pornography trial in which the imaginary accused novel took place in a woman's mind in the average length of time of a romantic encounter: seven minutes. Though Wallace wrote of an imaginary novel, there are many real novels like it.

You might argue that the important part of plots worked out this way actually cover more time than the premise, and you'd be right. After all, the escape in "An Occurrence at Owl Creek Bridge" takes up most of the story, not the hanging. However, the movement of the plot is from the victim's predicament (he is about to be hanged) through his struggle (mental) to his losing the struggle. That all is a matter of seconds. The fact that the readers experience various compressions and expansions of time is a question of how the plot is presented and not a question of the plot itself.

Ah, but those of you who favor science fiction might offer the following. A character goes into the past with a time machine. He goes back to medieval times. He has a hard time adjusting, but when the time comes for him to return to the present, he chooses to stay with the woman he loves. So, then, you might say, the plot isn't chronological. The character goes backward in time!

Sorry, you know better than that. The character is experiencing one thing following another. Whether he experiences this succession of things in different settings is irrelevant. "The past is another country," begins L. P. Hartley's beautiful novel *The Go-Between*, "they do things differently there." A character begins in one setting, say France in the present, and takes a time machine into another setting, say Burgundy in the twelfth century. It isn't any different than if he had taken a train from France to Belgium without a time machine. His story is still moving in one chronological direction. He is experiencing one thing after another.

To save confusion, I should also make another aspect of plot chronology quite clear. In many stories, the plot is presented non-chronologically. We experience parts of the plot out of the order in which they occurred. This has long been a technique of the novelist, though most novels are pretty straightforward in going from the beginning to the end. Movies, too, are usually in straight chronology, though films like *Pulp Fiction, Rashomon*, and Greta Gerwig's *Little Women* all rearrange scenes for particular purposes. Underlying these variations on presenting the plot is the plot itself. Such stories allow us to see the plot in a different way and reveal something about character or morality or whatever that might not be as obvious if the story were told in a chronological order.

Let me use the example of my own novel *Bloody Marko*. The protagonist is a Serb who suffers as a child and becomes (unlike most of his countrymen) a collaborator with the Nazi invaders in World War II. When the war ends, his skills as a torturer are used by the CIA in South America. He has become a monster, and when he gets too old to be useful, he is sent back to Communist Yugoslavia for trial as a war criminal. Basically, this is an outline of the plot.

However, I chose to begin my novel in the present and continue backwards through a succession of scenes to his childhood. My purpose in this scheme of telling the story in reverse chronological order was to reveal the horrible and amazing way in which things accumulate to create monsters. Marko becomes what he becomes because of the events of his life. I thought it would be more interesting to show him first as decrepit monster, then go back to show how he became one. In this way, I could play off what *appears* to have made him the way he is against what the reader later finds out really made him the way he is. The point is that underlying the storytelling method is a chronological plot. It begins with Marko's experiences as a boy in World War I and ends with his stroke at his war crimes trial. One event follows another, though the story is told in reverse.

THE CAUSAL CHAIN

But that isn't all there is to plot. Events happen in order every day. Time moves forward. This happens and that happens. Things happening don't necessarily make a plot.

Let's say Joe Blough wakes up a little early. He lies in bed until the alarm goes off. He gets up, showers, combs his beard, and eats cold pizza for breakfast. He climbs down the stairs in his apartment building and goes to his car, wiping a smudge off the windshield with his thumb. On his way to work, the traffic backs up. He sees a beautiful blonde in a Lexus who makes him feel guilty over a woman he broke up with two years ago. He knows he is happy with his current girlfriend, but he can't help but wonder what might have been. He thinks about the report he is supposed to finish before noon and hopes the correct statistics have been e-mailed to him as he was asked. He warns himself not to get caught up in the conversation around the coffee maker. Despite working hard, he doesn't finish the report on time, anyway, and his boss, tied up with interviewing applicants for a new receptionist says not to worry about it. The report is not really needed until Monday.

Does Joe Blough's life sound like anybody's life? Maybe yours? You can substitute male or female, different jobs, and different details, but it doesn't make for interesting reading. It's reality. It's experienced in chronological order, but it falls far short of being a story.

Why? It has no plot.

A second defining element of a plot is the causal chain. Events not only follow one another, they are related. An event causes the event that follows and it, in turn, causes the event that follows it. What caused Joe Blough to wake up early? Nothing. Often we wake up early and don't have any real reason for it. He could have awakened because of a noise in the next apartment: the Bickerfolks, who live next door, seem to argue twenty-four hours a day. Or maybe Joe was having a bad dream about the report he needed to finish. Or maybe he had a bad dream about his former girlfriend.

There could be a nearly infinite number of reasons why he woke up early, and each of them might become part of a plot. However, his waking up without a reason does not begin a causal chain.

Joe doesn't finish his report. What consequence results from his failure? Again, nothing. His boss says, "Well, it doesn't matter. I'm busy today. Monday will be soon enough." In this case we have a cause for many dramatic consequences. Suppose the boss is furious. Joe has been late before, but this time is the last straw. Joe is fired. It unhinges him. He gets a gun and shoots everyone in the office.

Or how about consequences not borrowed so blatantly from the news? Joe doesn't finish the report because he finds contradictions in the statistics which arrived late. A close examination of them indicates that someone has been manipulating them to conceal serious problems in another division of the company. Joe's alertness gets him promoted.

There could be a nearly infinite number of consequences from Joe's failure to finish the report. A plot requires that these consequences be causally related, however. The cleverer you are as a writer, the more interesting these causes and effects may be. The question of how believable these connections are will come into play, of course, and we will discuss that in more detail later in the book. When Joe eats the cold pizza for breakfast, it could be a stretch to say that is what causes him to wipe the stain off his windshield. When the traffic backs up, it would be a stretch to say that it was caused by Joe's waking up early. But it might be possible somehow to do it. Never underestimate your own imagination.

One of my favorite short stories is one by Bruce Jay Friedman in which a man makes an arbitrary choice, such as walking to work instead of taking the bus. It begins a chain of events that ends with his being fitted for a pair of cement overshoes. It all turns out to be a nightmare which he wakes up from. His wife then asks him whether he'd rather have sausage or bacon for breakfast, and the man is unable to choose because he senses that the most seemingly insignificant choice can begin a chain of events of life and death significance.

In the world of stories, that is how it should always work. In our lives often insignificant things may result in significant results. If the sausage is tainted with salmonella or beef byproducts infected with "mad cow" disease, choosing sausage over bacon may change our lives drastically. But most of the time it won't matter. The Puritans of the seventeenth century did not approve of many forms of writing, such as poetry, play writing, and fiction, but they did approve of diaries because the close examination of their own lives might reveal God's pattern for them. Many people do this in an informal way. They look back upon their time in this world and try to see the meaning of it. What are they doing but trying to make a plot of their lives?

If you read autobiographies and biographies, you will find much of this attempt to relate events by cause. This woman became the CEO of a digital corporation because she grew up in a home with strict rules. This fellow became the mogul of a fast-food empire because his parents were hippies without rules. Sir Isaac Newton was a genius because he had a terrible stepfather. Picasso was genius because he had a supportive father. If the causal relationships seem strained, they often are. When we look at factual history, we are often creating plots to explain the inexplicable.

The great English writer and courtier Sir Philip Sidney wrote *A Defence of Poetry* to counter Puritan objections to what we would call "fiction," the making up of stories. In his essay he addresses this very question by asking what it is that history teaches us. He gives the example of two Roman emperors named Severus. One was cruel and evil; the other good. The evil Severus prospered and died of old age at age 65. The good Severus at age 27 was murdered by his own soldiers. It is hard to make any sort of lesson out of this. Stuff happens. To make stories out of stuff, we must reshape it so that there are cause and effect relationships.

Ever notice how people stand around at funerals and discuss why the deceased died? Lying there is the casket was a person of some sort—good, bad, ugly, happy, kind, cruel, or stupid—and the funeral guests may blame the person for eating too much or smoking (causing the fatal heart attack or cancer), driving without glasses, loving too much and bringing on a broken heart, or having had the bad luck of being born into a genetically bad family. It is so inconceivable that a living, breathing person should die that we want and need an explanation for it, a cause. The fact that it might not have a cause that can be determined is very disturbing.

Our need for this is also for me (and I speak strictly for myself here) illustrated in such terrible events as the assassination of John F. Kennedy. Young and handsome, he filled the nation with hope and pride. The fact that a disturbed individual with a rifle could end the president's life in the way that he did is so fundamentally unsettling, that it spawned a huge industry in concocting theories (plotlines) for the event. At various times, the CIA, Fidel Castro, the Mafia, the Soviet secret police, the lunatic right wing, and even Lyndon Johnson have been accused of arranging the assassination. Yet, nothing has ever been revealed of any significance which indicates anything other than that Lee Harvey Oswald fired out the book depository window and struck down the president. We don't want to believe such an arbitrary event could change history so profoundly. So, we make up a story with the required cause and effect elements. Similarly, there have been conspiracy theories about the deaths of Marilyn Monroe, Martin Luther King, Jr., Princess Diana, Jeffrey Epstein, and you-name-them. Such deaths seem so emotionally unacceptable, that their must be a reason behind it. It gives us comfort to create a cause and effect relationship, even if one is not clear. That's why stories are always so much more satisfying than the news.

Let's look at another example to help us understand exactly what a plot consists of. The following is a quotation from English Renaissance writer George Herbert (1593-1633):

> For want of a nail the shoe is lost, for want of a shoe the horse is lost, for want of a horse the rider is lost.

You may recognize this warning about the consequences of neglect as having been borrowed by Benjamin Franklin for his *Poor Richard's Almanac*. Later writers also elaborated it and said "for want of the rider, the battle was lost."

Okay, it's a good quotation, but does it meet the requirements to be a plot? I would say it does. First, it is in chronological order. There are four events which follow one upon the other. Someone neglected to put in the full number of nails. A nail is missing and the horseshoe falls off. The missing shoe incapacitates the horse. The incapacitated horse takes the rider out of the race or battle or whatever it is the rider is up to.

The quotation also meets the second defining aspect of a plot because the events are related to each other causally. If the nail were not missing, presumably the horseshoe would not have fallen off. If the shoe were on the horse, it would not have been incapacitated. And so on. The causal aspect is very important in this mini-plot because it implies the theme, which is that there can be large consequences of small oversights.

INCREASING INTENSITY

Having decided that this quotation is a plot also reveals another aspect of plotting that is essential. A plot is a chronological series of events with a causal relation to each other. As in a line of carefully arranged dominoes, the first event causes the second to fall and the second causes the third to fall, and so on. However, for a plot to be effective, the intensity of each event must be greater than the last.

When a long line of dominoes falls, each domino falls in the same way as the last one. However, when we see those attempts to break the Guinness world record we see how the dominoes are arranged to produce special effects, such as spiraling up ramps, different colored dominoes are interwoven to make patterns such as flags, and so on. The interest in these thousands of dominoes falling increases because of these nifty tricks, but on the very basic levels it is the sheer number of dominoes falling which increases the intensity. Each one that falls moves us closer to the objective, which is to break the Guinness record.

Let's go back to Joe Blough, real life guy, as our example. Joe wakes up early and because he wakes up early, he nicks himself shaving. Because he nicks himself shaving, he searches for a Band-Aid and only finds a damp one. Because it is all he can find, he uses it. Because it is damp, it falls off on his drive to work.

Does the word "yawn" sum this up? The series of events is in chronological order. They have been causally related to each other. Unfortunately, however, there is no significant increase in intensity. The voltage goes up a notch when Joe nicks himself, but after that, though each event is caused by the previous, there is no real increase in the danger, consequences, or meaning of what happens. It doesn't matter that Joe nicked himself shaving. It might cause a number of things, but it does not lead to anything that matters.

It isn't important that the first event in the chain of events be obviously consequential, but it must lead directly to meaningful consequences. Mighty oaks grow from little acorns, eh? Joe could bleed to death because he nicks his carotid! Joe's nick could become infected with the flesh-eating bacteria, which destroys his face and his job in public relations! The nick could, for some reason, congeal all the distaste Joe's girlfriend has been developing for him, provoking her to dump him! These consequences are excessive and probably incredible, but you get the point. The intensity increases.

You might know the poem by William Butler Yeats called "Leda and the Swan" which brilliantly meditates on the unforseen consequences of a small act. As in the myth, Zeus takes on the form of a swan to seduce Leda. Because of this, Helen of Troy is born, which through a series of events leads to the bloodshed of war and the destruction of the great city of Troy. This romantic interlude, a relatively insignificant thing, brings about the end of a civilization. Each step in the story of how the Trojan War came about has greater and greater consequences.

But the world doesn't have to come to an end in a plot because of the chain of events. In fact, the world doesn't even have to be threatened, as it is in many thrillers. The chain of events could be strictly emotional and limited to a single character. The intensity can internal, as it is in many literary stories. A woman comes to understand the cruelty of the world. A man recognizes he is incapable of real love. The rule is, however, that in the context of the story, the consequence of each event in the chain must be more intense than the events it follows.

RISING ACTION

Ideally, each link in the causal chain should be higher in intensity than the previous. What do I mean by that? It seems self-evident: of course stories should get more exciting as we move through them! The real question is how you go about doing it. One of the adages of the old pulp writers was, "Get your hero in trouble and keep him there." A plot needs a central problem for the main character to struggle with. The protagonist needs something and is going to try to get it. Maybe Dirk needs to find the treasure of the Incas. Maybe Emily needs to find out who murdered her accountant. Maybe Mr. Buddwing (an amnesiac) needs to find out who he is. Or maybe Janetta needs to reconcile herself with her father.

It must be a problem the audience can identify with. This is not always very clear cut. If James Bond is trying to save the Free World from Dr. No's evil scheme, it may seem ludicrous initially. Yet, if the story develops properly the audience will want the debonair Bond to succeed. The audience will admire Bond's sexiness and intelligence; they will fantasize being Bond saving the world. On the other hand, many young writers use their own experiences in love as the subject of fiction. Almost everyone has gone through the experience of being disappointed in love. So we should be thoroughly able to identify with a real world problem like being dumped by a lover.

Unfortunately, what we find when we read many such stories is that they leave us cold. Maybe it's the "been there, done that" phenomenon. Exactly because we've so many of us been disappointed in love at age sixteen (and probably would prefer not to be reminded of it), there needs to be some additional dimension to the story that makes it more compelling. After all, we survived being dumped by Lola or Lyle, later met a partner far more lovable, and moved on. All of the anguish of losing Lola or Lyle now seems a bit overdone. The consequences of the struggle are not very significant unless elements such as those in Shakespeare's *Romeo and Juliet*, or William Inge's *Splendor in the Grass*, or Nicholas Sparks's novel *The Notebook* heighten the drama. We have a sense in most stories of juvenile love that the characters might be in trouble, but they're not going to stay in trouble.

The first requirement of increasing intensity is, therefore, creating a connection between the audience and the protagonists, whether those characters are as fantastical as James Bond, the Elephant Man, Peter Pan, or the rabbits in *Watership Down*, or as real as the characters in S. E. Hinton's *The Outsiders*, John Le Carré's *Smiley's People*, or James Baldwin's *Go Tell It on the Mountain*. If we don't care about the main characters, we won't care about their problems.

Aristotle observes that we all hate to see a good person suffer and a bad person prosper, and then goes on to say that the main character should be good. In most instances, this is true. More stories are a struggle between "good guys" and "bad guys." Our definitions of good and bad may vary greatly, but the audience wants to root for people it believes to be good and hiss those who aren't. Our sense of psychological realism usually requires that our good guys have some negative traits and our bad guys some positive ones. It's hard to believe in, let alone feel a connection with, a character who is invincible, always pure of heart, or who never makes a mistake. Readers want good characters, but they cannot identify with characters that have no humanity.

Some writers have made evil characters their main characters with wonderful results. A lot of the audience interest then becomes "How will good stop this monster?" Yet, when such stories succeed, the bad character often earns audience fascination for his or her intelligence, cleverness, and charm. Often the author makes the audience feel the torments that drove the bad character to evil. If you look at the facts, Jesse James was a common homicidal felon, but movies and books show him outwitting the law, acting out of revenge against the railroads or against carpetbaggers. He is handsome. He is in love. He's nice to his mother. He seems more sinned against than sinning. The audience begins to like him and hope he doesn't get caught.

I don't want to go into a whole discussion of characterization here. That deserves a book in itself. Later there will be a chapter devoted to the relationship between character and plot. Suffice it here to say that if we wish our plots to have a feeling of increasing intensity, then we've got to make our readers care about what happens to the main characters. Our readers may identify with the main characters by fantasizing having their superhuman qualities, or by thinking they personally have those qualities. "If I could leap tall buildings, I would fight crime, too," they think. Or "I, too, would give a hungry child my last dollar." And as to bad characters, who hasn't imagined embezzling a million bucks from a heartless corporation, or asked themselves what would make them capable of committing murder?

The second requirement of rising action is that the problem is a significant one. Significance, as we've seen above is as ambiguous as "identifying." Within the context of the story, however, the failure to solve the problem must seem to promise disaster. Achilles' anger in *The Iliad* means nothing unless it may cause the Greeks to lose the war (which it nearly does). If the German spy in *Eye of the Needle* is allowed to get his message back to Berlin, the Normandy invasion will fail and Europe will remain under Nazi rule. But it can be made as significant in a novel that a woman might fail to catch the affection of Mr. Darcy or Rochester (the man she loves) and be condemned to either a loveless marriage or a lonely "spinsterhood."

Both of these requirements are related to plot, but are not necessarily the direct product of it. The third requirement, however, is very much a result of how the plot is built. Increasing intensity implies a progression through time and the passage of time is certainly an aspect of plotting. Getting protagonists in trouble doesn't require the passage of time (except in setting it up), but keeping them in trouble does.

Novels progress by building scene upon scene, piling them upon the previous scenes causally. To increase intensity, the scenes must move to a more important, more dangerous level as they evolve. Simultaneously, the main character must be trapped in a tighter and tighter situation. The possibilities for action are getting narrower and narrower. The number of choices the character has available get smaller, until he or she is faced with two choices—quite often, take a horrible risk or die.

So we might consider plots to be like a cone which characters are moving through from the wide end to the narrow. It closes in the further along they go. Or we might also consider plots to be like a bracket chart for a sports tournament. Where the characters begin their struggle with the problem, there are many options. As the tournament progresses, teams are eliminated. Similarly, as characters move through each level of the story there are fewer and fewer choices until we come to the last one at the story's resolution.

Do you recall Edgar Allan Poe's short story "The Pit and the Pendulum"? In it, a man is confined to a dungeon during the Inquisition. He is tied to a platform and a large pendulum with a knife-like blade is swinging above him, dropping closer and closer. He appears to be doomed, but he rubs the ropes holding him with the terrible meat they had been feeding him and the rats gnaw him free. His captors aren't finished yet, however. The walls of the room in which he is confined are heated red hot and begin to close in on him, pushing him towards the edge of a deadly pit. He will be burned to death or fall to his death. At the last possible moment to save him, General LaSalle, a previously unintroduced character, reaches in to snatch him to safety. Poe was a master of building intensity, and we forgive him the obvious *deus ex machina* of General LaSalle because of that intensity. Consider how the narrator of "The Tell-Tale Heart" is driven by his conscience to the point that he can no longer resist confessing, or how "The Fall of the House of Usher" builds to the "resurrection" of Roderick Usher's sister. Until we can build such intensity, the rest of us should be more careful with such cheap endings.

Let's use an example of a simple detective story to further illustrate how a plot increases intensity. Dick Gumshoe is in his office when Elaine Mysterioso comes in. She wants him to find her ex-husband. Dick, at this point, could choose to do any number of things. There isn't much consequence if he refuses to take the case, though, of course, there wouldn't be a story if he refused.

He takes the case and now must choose how to search for the ex-husband. He can call a friend at the police department. He can check with the shoeshine guy about the "word on the street." He can visit the last place Elaine saw her ex-husband and question the neighbors. Whichever he chooses, he will be led in a particular direction and, if the plot is intensifying, he will have fewer choices. He will meet harsher and harsher obstacles. At first, people warn him off with words, then they threaten him physically, then they beat him up, and then maybe they do something that really hurts Dick Gumshoe, such as murdering his favorite bartender.

In the end, perhaps, he finds the ex-husband is a prisoner on a trawler in the harbor. If Dick Gumshoe calls the Coast Guard, the bad guys will probably just toss the man into the furnace before he can be rescued. Dick Gumshoe's only choice is to sneak on board and attempt to rescue him. Of course, this is the most dangerous moment in the plot for Dick Gumshoe, and his choice is life or death.

If you think about this, you will see it happening in every sort of story. How many times did Captain Kirk demand even more power from the overloaded engines of the starship Enterprise? They're either going to blow up, or lose. Losing is not an option for the captain, though Scotty isn't as certain: "I'm giving her all I can, captain!"

How many thrillers come down to choosing which of two wires must be cut to stop the doomsday device from going off? And how many love stories come down to the woman trusting her feelings one more time and choosing to believe the man no one else believes?

PLOT AND STORY

Let's go back to the George Herbert quotation. Obviously it adheres to the requirements of a plot in building intensity, also. Each step creates a greater consequence until the rider is lost.

But if our quotation is a plot, is it also a story? Of course not. It is stripped of almost everything other than plot that makes a story interesting. It has a few details—the nail, the horse, the rider—and it has thematic content. It also has diction. If it weren't worded well, it wouldn't be a well-known quotation. What it lacks, however, are setting and character. We don't know what horse, what kind of horse, the time period, the circumstances that make the rider's task important, who the rider is, what kind of person the rider is, nor what is lost by the rider's being put out of action. These particularities would change the meaning of the story quite drastically.

For instance, if we set the story in the American Civil War, we might have a Confederate blacksmith, Hieronymus Cracker, short of nails. He decides to leave off one of the nails for a courier's horse. An urgent message needs to be sent between General Robert E. Lee and General Braxton Bragg about the situation near Chattanooga and the possibility of reinforcements. The rider, Gaylord Taliaferro, sets out at a fast gallop. His steed, Caesar, throws a shoe and falls. Caesar's leg is broken and Taliaferro is thrown. When he regains consciousness, he is forced to put Caesar to sleep. The sound of the shot draws the attention of a Union patrol and Taliaferro is captured. The urgent message never gets through and General Bragg is uncertain how to proceed, losing a great opportunity to inflict damage on the Union.

Or, let's concoct our story around something more romantic. Reuben Sandwich of Cherry Grove, Tennessee, is in love with Emeline Skirt, a daughter of his family's enemies. The Skirts and the Sandwiches have been feuding since the hills were settled. He and she decide they cannot live without each another. Emeline is soon with child, and they decide to elope. He will ride through the night to her family's side of the mountain to meet her at Moonshine Peak. As twilight falls, he sees that his horse Charleston has thrown a shoe. He tries to repair it after dark when his parents won't hear, but he does it in a rush and does not put in all the nails. On his way to his rendezvous, the horseshoe comes loose and Charleston plummets into a ravine. Reuben barely saves his life by clutching a branch, but now has to run to his love. It takes so long that Emeline despairs and throws herself off the peak. Reuben cries out in anguish and is shot by Emeline's brother, who has been out looking for her with his bloodhounds.

As presented here, these two stories are not likely to attract the notice of the Nobel Prize Committee. You will notice, however, how very different they seem. It might take someone who wasn't looking for the underlying structure quite a while to recognize that they are both built upon the same basic plot structure. And, remember, most readers don't give much thought to plot structure, even if they know what it is. Most readers are interested in the story, not how it is constructed.

Writers, however, must think differently. If you want to be a writer, you'll have to learn to think like one. The painter may consider dozens of compositional and color theories in creating a canvas, while the viewers merely "know what they like.". The musician may contemplate various ways of orchestrating, timing, and key shifting to complete a song, while listeners want to know if it's easy listening or heavy metal. To become a good writer, you must similarly become aware of story patterns and structures. Quite often, a flaw in the plot will reveal exactly what you need to change in order to make your novel stand proud.

BRAINSTORMER #2

Take a novel you admire, the kind of book you'd like to write: romance, horror, whatever.

Write a plot outline of it. Remember to keep it in chronological order, as opposed to story order.

Note the relationship between consecutive steps in the plot, how one event causes the next. If you find any weak causal connections, think about why they are weak. Ask yourself how these weaknesses could be repaired.

Chapter 3
The Plot Outline

Pardon a bit of history here, but a little background might help explain why so many contemporary writers dismiss the outline as a poor way to go about creating a novel. There is a myth of creativity which has been with us since ancient times, but was articulated most forcefully in the Romantic movement of the late 18th and 19th centuries and has stuck with us through two centuries.

Romantics rebelled against the Neoclassical idea that art was a systematic structuring of balanced effects. Romantics thought that true art came from a heart freed of the rules of composition and structure, or from the unembellished reality of the world. Edgar Allan Poe and Mary Shelley searched the dark corridors of the mind and the extremes of the emotion. Walter Scott and Victor Hugo looked for the heroism in common people, while George Eliot, Balzac, and Charles Dickens, incorporated keen observations of the world about them. They freed the arts from formulas that had become outdated and introduced more spontaneity.

At the beginning of the "rebellion," the artists were well trained in Classical forms, so that when they stepped over the line it was both outrageous and immensely refreshing. Later artists stepped further over the line and created a new line which other artists stepped over, and so on. Originality and vigor became the primary values in art, and formal considerations became less important in the minds of creative people.

By the twentieth century artists strove for absolute freedom. Painting became abstract; music introduced random, non-instrumental sounds; and novelists distorted the conventions of language itself, as in James Joyce's *Finnegans Wake*. This soon produced the impression, as the cliché goes, that the pendulum had swung too far, but the general enthusiasm for creative freedom remains in place.

Inspiration, we are told, is the key to writing well. Inspiration is The Force. Once you are inspired, the perfect words pour from your fingers. How nice if it were true! Inspiration would be far more impressive as a theory of creation if we did not know how hard writers actually work. Authors cover their manuscripts with insertions, deletions, and cross-outs. Word processors conceal that evidence with the writer's friend, the Delete button, but the many different drafts in literary archives demonstrate that little writing that is truly good comes out spontaneously.

Ask any professional. Waiting for inspiration does not put words on paper. Writers will tell you that writing is work and must be approached as work. Most writers have a regular writing schedule, having discovered that the Muse is fickle. She tends to drop in—if at all—when you are already writing.

Nonetheless, belief in inspiration and in originality is part of the reason that plotting and outlining are dismissed as inhibiting. An outline doesn't allow the heart to pursue its impulses, goes the conventional wisdom. Reality is not structured, goes the argument, why should art that imitates reality be structured? Structured art is sterile, the argument goes, despite the many great novels that prove that a tight structure handled well produces great emotional and realistic power. How many great literary works were written in totalitarian nations or under societal pressures, such as obscenity laws? Outlining seems like no restriction when compared to the rack or a firing squad.

THE APPRENTICE'S TOOLBOX

Yet, the myth that outlining is a bad idea is still perpetuated by authors. Part of it is the logic of the arguments above: "Outlines are not creative. I am creative. I do not use an outline." Another part of it is that the authors who give advice to you, a beginning author, have often forgotten what it is to be a beginning author. Authors giving advice have managed to survive writing at least one novel. They have seen many of the pitfalls and misjudgments that befuddle the beginning novelist. They have developed habits for writing and have some confidence in them. Most importantly, they know that they can get through the process. They know what they are up against, but know they can make it to the end. This is not to say they find the process of writing easy or that they always know what to do and how to do it. But they have a reached a level of confidence which beginning novelists cannot have.

Think of a child learning to throw a ball. How silly it can look! The ball falls out before the hand moves forward. The ball goes the opposite direction it is intended. It pops up in the air and bops the kid on the head. Yet, once a child has learned the movements, there is little thought involved. No longer does the placement of the fingers need to be remembered. Now the kid concentrates on hitting the target, striking out the batter, casting the ball as far and as high as possible.

The beginning novelist is like a child who has not yet found out where to place the fingers. Different people throw a ball differently, but each, through practice, finds the most comfortable and effective way. An accomplished novelist never stops learning, but is learning on a different level. Many of the fundamentals have become automatic.

One of these fundamentals is plotting. Many accomplished novelists never outlined. They wrote, rewrote, restructured, and rewrote again and again until they got it right. They have learned to plot in their heads. Some say they don't know how their novels are going to end when they begin them, but most, when pressed, will admit they have at least a vague ending in mind, even if the middle is not clear. They may change the ending later when they realize it doesn't fit the logical progression of the plot, but they have at least a crude plot in mind when they begin. Most probably have a more precise plot in mind than many other writers create on paper.

Most professional writers make notes and sketch out their ideas informally on paper before they begin. Others are lucky enough to have contracts for future books and must provide the publishers with some sort of outline for the novels they are planning. Mystery writer Elizabeth George is reputed to be a very careful outliner, who does not begin her books until they are carefully mapped out. Carolyn G. Hart, another popular mystery writer, says she finds writing a detailed outline frustrating, but usually thinks out the totality of the book before she begins. Polish science fiction writer Stanislaw Lem once said that he did not begin a book until he had an ending in mind because he once found himself stuck without an ending. Writing a novel is too much work to arrive at a dead end with only an unfinished manuscript to show for it.

In the movie business, writers outline (in what is called a "treatment") until the producers think the general story structure is workable. Afterwards the screenplay is written, which is really only a blue print for a motion picture. Why so much outlining before filming? Because making movies costs millions of dollars. You don't just grab a camera crew and a few actors and start filming. You'd be burning money at a phenomenal rate. Now maybe your "pay" as a novelist is minuscule compared to a union "best boy" on a film, but isn't your time valuable? Regularly published novelists take their time seriously. If you want to be a novelist, you must take yourself as seriously as if you have a million bucks riding on it. After all, you really might.

THE PROCESS OF OUTLINING

As I discussed in the first chapter, there are many aspects of a novel: word choice, characterization, and the others. All of these work in combination in a good novel. The plot will make sense given the behavior of the characters, for example, or the rhythm of the prose conveys a strong sense of mood and place. However, juggling all these aspects can be very confusing. If there is a way to concentrate on one aspect at a time, it will make the overwhelming nature of the work in front of you seem less forbidding.

Think of it. As you're writing in the middle of your chapter one, you've got one eye on the sentence in which you are trying to say that Ralph Schlump has developed a foot fungus and the other eye on how this sentence affects the scene. Then one of your eyes flicks away to check how this scene affects the ending you've planned, and—oh no!—if Schlump has a foot fungus, will that make his impersonator easy to identify by the pool at the Hotel Ritz. Soon, you're tearing your hair out, despairing of your ability to write at all.

Divide the work and conquer. If you were painting the Sistine Chapel, you'd first work out an overall design. That settled, you could concentrate on each panel of the design. That settled, you could concentrate on how you intend to paint God's finger extended toward Adam's. You'd be able to concentrate on one thing at a time.

Outlining allows you to concentrate on what I like to call the "macrobook." The macrobook is the overall design of the novel. Say you want a novel that begins with a frantic crowd scene, then gradually closes in on an individual in the crowd and examines her life in great detail, and then ends with her being swallowed in the crowd again. Or you want a novel that begins late in the plot with the body of a missing man washing up on shore, then proceeds to go through a series of *Citizen Kane*-like vignettes in which we discover who this man was and in the final scene, who killed him. The macrobook is your novel viewed from a distance, so that you can see the whole thing. You are concerned with its strategy, not its tactics. You think about overall effect and thus, its structure.

The structure or plot of your novel is the foundation upon which it is built, but your novel is made up of much smaller units. You choose a name for a character. You decide whether he shall stutter and how much. You determine how long the victim lay dying before being discovered by the police and why. The most important part of putting together these smaller units (doing the "microbook"), however, is the actual assembling of phrases and sentences. Will you call this character "chubby" or "abdominous"? Will you say, "Rodney threw his shoes across the room in disgust" or "Rodney's shoes thumped against the wall and he shook with anger"?

Many writers do a quick first draft to create the macrobook, then go back to concentrate on the quality of the microbook, editing meticulously. Everyone knows how one wrong sentence can ruin a page or one wrong word can turn a sentence from brilliant to laughable. "The difference between the right word and the nearly right word is the same as that between the lightning and the lightning bug," Mark Twain warns us. There is a great deal of pressure in this meticulous work of the microbook. One word-brick at a time. One line at a time.

Being able to devote full attention to the microbook without confusing yourself with issues of the macrobook can be a distinct advantage. Once you have created a clear conception of your macrobook, you will better know your objective in each scene and be able to concentrate on making lightning rather than lightning bugs.

CREATING THE CHAIN OF EVENTS

"So, okay," you say, "you've convinced me to try it. How in the world do I do an outline?"

First, break down your story idea into separate scenes. Begin at the beginning of the chain of events and briefly sketch out each step in the progression of events. The first event in the chain of events will not necessarily be your first scene in the novel, but at this point don't worry about it. Your plot outline might look something like this:

1) Zeus takes the form of a swan to seduce Leda
2) Leda gives birth to Helen of Troy, the most beautiful woman on earth.
3) When Helen reaches marrying age, all the princes of Greece come to court her. In order to guarantee that her marriage is not threatened by one of the losing suitors, they all agree to defend her choice. She chooses Menelaus.
4) Three goddesses, Athena, Aphrodite, and Hera, ask Prince Paris of Troy to choose who among them is most beautiful. Each goddess tries to bribe him, but Aphrodite promises him the most beautiful woman on earth. Paris chooses Aphrodite.
5) Paris goes to Sparta, meets and seduces Helen, and flees with her back to Troy.

6) The princes of Greece hold true to their oath and set out with a great army to restore Helen to her husband.
7) The war drags on for a decade, with many great warriors falling as casualties.
8) The Greeks conceive a plan to feign a complete withdrawal and leave behind a wooden statue of a horse as a supposed offering.
9) The Trojans drag the horse inside the walls and the Greeks concealed in the horse's belly, sneak out and open the city gates.
10) The Greek army pours in and in a fit of brutality, slaughters and pillages the great city and leaves it an empty ruin.

You will recognize this plot outline as being from ancient Greek and Roman literature and mythology. Different parts of the story are told in various sources, including *The Iliad*, *The Odyssey*, and *The Aeneid*. No one ancient source tells the entire story, though this is the overall plot of which we might be intending to make a novel.

Each step of our outline is in chronological order and we can see how each step is caused by the previous. Each step is also more intense than the last, resulting in a spectacular ending with fire and carnage.

If we were to use this plot outline completely, however, we can see much trouble in store. This novel would be enormous. In summarizing it here I have skipped over many, many details, not to mention the many things any imaginative person could add to it. The plot could be extended to include such things as the murder of King Agamemnon by Queen Clytemnestra when he returned from the war, the ten year quest of Odysseus to reach home, or the flight of the Trojan Aeneas to the shores of Italy, where his descendants Romulus and Remus found Rome. You might add such consequences as what Helen and Menelaus' marriage was like after she returned to Sparta or how the Trojan slaves adapted to their new masters.

If this plot is to be one novel, it is either going to be a huge, multi-volume one, or it will be superficial, barely touching the possible

Mastering Plot

power of a moment such as when Helen walks on the walls of Troy to see the battle she is responsible for. The entire *Iliad,* an epic poem of about 600 pages in a modern translation by Robert Fagles, covers only a tiny part of our step 7) above. *The Iliad* is concerned only with an episode involving Achilles' anger over being shortchanged in the looting of slaves and the consequences of it on the war effort.

In *The Poetics,* Aristotle raises the question of the magnitude of a story. If the story is too big, he says, it is like an animal a thousand miles long. It becomes impossible to get any sense of it because it is too overwhelming. He then tells us the genius of Homer was that he understood this and did not tell the entire story. He selected a small part of it that might represent the whole. Aristotle was concerned, of course, with the magnitude of a dramatic plot, but the epic poem, especially as represented by Homer's works, comes very close in needing a magnitude similar to that of a novel. Some novels have greater magnitude than others, just as *The Odyssey* has greater magnitude than *The Iliad,* but most novels and epic poems have much greater magnitude than a story suitable for a drama.

So then, if we look at our plot outline above, it should be immediately obvious what difficulty we'd have in stuffing all of that into the normal size of a novel. If we did not look at such a plot outline, we might happily begin with Leda being leered at by Zeus and after a month of writing we'd still have Helen in diapers.

SEEING PROBLEMS

If I had not borrowed an extensive plot from Greek mythology, but had made up one, there would likely be other problems that might show themselves as structural defects in our hypothetical novel. Managing to chart out the steps in chronological order shouldn't be a problem, though sometimes writers run into a problem by getting details, such as the age or time period of a character confused. Normally, unless your plot is very complex, the chronology should be rather straightforward.

The causal relationships between steps, however, might not be so straightforward. Remember that each step is a domino intended to fall against the next. In many routine hard-boiled detective novels, the beginning of *The Maltese Falcon* is borrowed and adapted. A woman comes into the detective's office and asks him to look for someone who's missing. It is the beginning of a chain of events. It causes the detective to begin the journey to finding the missing person.

There isn't much difficulty in setting this situation up so that the woman's visit causes what follows. The detective needs money. The blonde is very attractive and the detective is—of course—a he-man who is stimulated by her. These factors become part of the detective's characterization. Later he can be tempted by money, sex, or both. However, the beginning of the search necessarily comes from the visit.

It would be quite a different story if the detective refused to take the job, or if the woman discovered his fee was more than she could pay and he refused to lower his price. It would be a very different story if the detective were rich, didn't need the job, didn't trust the woman, didn't do missing persons, or was in love with his male partner and found no attraction in women. In that case, he wouldn't necessarily take on the job, and if he did, the plot would need other compelling factors to make him go to work.

A few examples from motion pictures (whose plots are not as subtle as those in many books) make the principle of necessity more obvious. Nearly everyone finds it amusing that in horror movies a lonely, frightened woman will investigate a strange noise by going down into the dark basement during a lightning storm when there is no necessity for her to do it. I was once in a theater in which a man yelled at the screen, "Yo, lady! Try 911!" She didn't, of course, and the creature made hash of her.

The woman's action in such films is not necessary and therefore seems like the writers are forcing the plot to go where they want, whether the cause is sufficient or not. If we were to ask, "Why did Mrs. Deadmeat go into the basement?" we'd get the answer "Because she heard a noise." We'd know, however, that going down there is not the necessary event to follow the noise without some further justification. It's not probable that a frightened person would do it.

So, additional factors make it more probable. She's been looking for her cat and mistakes the noise for Fluffy. She's a tough, ex-Marine who thinks she can handle anything. She can't call the cops because she's justly or unjustly wanted for murder. The phones are out at the farm and her husband has the pickup truck. Anything like this makes her behavior more causally related to what motivates it. Notice how many mysteries take place in lonely mansions cut off by a storm, making the solving of the mystery necessary by the people who are trapped. The murderer is one of the guests, but they can't simply call the police.

Perhaps the best example of how to get a character into the cellar where the murderer lurks is in the plotline of Alfred Hitchcock's *Psycho*. Past midway in the film, a private detective enters the Bates house searching for evidence relating to the disappearance of Marion Crane. The audience knows a murderer lurks inside, but the detective doesn't. His actions seem logical because Norman Bates acted like he was hiding something. When he is murdered, he fails to return a call to his client, Marion Crane's sister. The sister then goes to the house to question the woman the detective mentioned in his last call. The woman isn't in her bedroom. Suddenly Norman is returning to the house, and the sister cannot get out the front door without being seen. She has no place to hide and sees the basement door. She hurries into the basement where she encounters Mrs. Bates in the breathtaking climax and barely escapes becoming the movie's third victim.

All of this has clear causal connections. The local sheriff won't help the sister go into the house. Marion's sister doesn't know the real condition of Mrs. Bates in the house. The sister has no knowledge of the stabbing of the detective. For all these reasons she has no fear of going down into the basement. It is a necessity for her to do so if she wishes to talk to Mrs. Bates and find out what happened to Marion.

The best motion picture scripts are very tight in the causal relationships between events and have to be simpler than novels because of the time factor. As screenwriter William Goldman said, a script is an express train moving from A to B, whereas the novel often digresses from the main track. Along the main track, though, the chain of causal relationships in a novel should be as tight as they are in a script. The appropriate digression can be very effective, but the key word here is "appropriate." A causally related event is always appropriate because it gets us further down the chain to the ending.

Digressions are appropriate only if they highly enrich the characterization, the tone, or the atmosphere. If you have any doubt about the importance of the digression, you should leave it out. Don't flatter yourself that you're such a powerful writer you can get away with a lengthy digression. Most often your novel will not suffer for lack of it, and contemporary readers are not as tolerant of descriptive or analytical digressions as they used to be. A description of Paris in the spring of 1957 may well enrich a novel, but generally your audience wants to know *what happened* there. Who shot Jean Le Mort and what made Inspector LeSnoup seek the murderer?

That's what readers want to know. Several pages of Inspector LeSnoup's trauma as a child when he found a body floating in the Seine had better reveal a great deal about his dogged determination to solve this unrelated crime, or it should be dropped. If the earlier murder causally relates to the later, no problem. If it is merely to demonstrate the inspector's character, his actions will usually speak much louder than the digression.

There is yet another reason in our time that adhering to the model of motion picture plotting can improve your novel's chances at success. It is a practical and pragmatic reason. The primary modes of storytelling in our society are the visual media. Certainly television and motion pictures dominate all other modes, including fiction and drama. There are many people who watch and never read. These are of no concern to you. But there is almost no one out there who reads but never watches. Even your most faithful readers will have, since

53

an early age, been trained to receive stories in the visual mode. Old-fashioned, rangy novels are rapidly disappearing as editors look for tight, quick novels. The best way to be tight and quick is to create an unbreakable causal chain.

COINCIDENCE

When we adhere to the rule that a plot has a strict causal chain, we immediately run into the problem of coincidence. The possibility of certain events taking place are so statistically minuscule that we would normally think they were impossible. Yet, such things do occur and we marvel at them. To make an unusual event into a coincidence, not only must the odds be long, there must be additional factors. *Someone* will win the Powerball lottery and receive a great pile of cash—that's not even unusual— but if a secondary factor comes into play, then it becomes a coincidence. As the numbers are announced, the winner, Damon Luckirump, has just found out his mother needs an operation. Or he wins the lottery on his birthday. The odds of Thomas Jefferson and John Adams dying on the same day are long, but not all that long. However they both died on the Fourth of July, 1826, fifty years after the date which we celebrate the signing of the Declaration of Independence and the birth of the United States. There seems to be a divine hand behind such a conjunction of factors.

In our day to day lives there are many examples of remarkable coincidences. Yet, as science fiction writer Stanislaw Lem once observed, the odds against being killed by lightning are meaningless if it happens to you. The Zippo lighter manufacturers had an advertising campaign based on supposedly true coincidental stories. A man who dropped his Zippo off the rail of a troop ship in 1945. Fifteen years later he lands a big swordfish off the Florida Keys. Guess what's in its belly? The Zippo, of course, and it still lights!

Often we try to explain away coincidences, which is a sign that we are suspicious of them—and a warning to those of us who want to use them in a plot. Maybe the guy in the ad mistook someone else's Zippo for his own, or Zippo made the thing up for advertising purposes. Sometimes we go such a long way in rationalizing a coincidence that is more elaborate than just allowing it to be a coincidence. In the notorious Bermuda Triangle there are the strange coincidences of disappearing ships and aircraft. Aliens did it, say some. A magnetic irregularity which might pull ships through time, say others. Ask the Coast Guard, however, and they will tell you these things aren't even coincidences. The sea traffic in that area is enormous and crowded with numbskull amateurs who retired to Florida and bought a yacht. The number of disappearances isn't even unusual, considering these factors.

But the Coast Guard's explanation—the sensible one, the true one—is the least fun of all the explanations. We like to feel that there is some thread pulling together what seem to be accidental occurrences, if we only knew enough science or the gods' intentions. And so we seek the hidden cause of events, particularly peculiar ones. One of my grandmother's favorite sayings was, "The Lord moves in mysterious ways, His wonders to perform." It was her explanation for any coincidences that seemed odd, and most of us settle for some similar explanation.

Amazing coincidences entertain us because they seem to reveal some kind of rationale in the random texture of ordinary life. We often feel there must be more to life than what we can see, and perhaps coincidences hint at this hidden order. Just when you think you've gotten everything figured out, here comes something weird. So what are we writers to do about coincidence? Is using them forbidden? Or is using them a way of replicating life's weird turns? It all rests on the question of credibility.

CREDIBILITY

When we're rolling along with a good story of some kind, we enjoy the feel of life in it. By this I don't mean that all we want is total realism. What we accept in a story varies according to the context. Unicorns are fine in fantasy novels. They'd be unusual, to say the least, in a police procedural and would require some pretty impressive writing for us to accept them. James Thurber's wonderful story, "The Unicorn in the Garden," has one, we think, until we get to the end and discover the story is not about something fantastical, but about a trick. Vampires have changed according to the fashions of the time: from being strictly the undead, to romantic fantasies, to psychologically tormented souls. If you think about it, it's a pretty funny notion that one type of vampire seems more real than another, but we often think that, don't we?

The reality we expect in a particular type of story isn't literal, therefore. We expect a story to operate within certain rules which we recognize as being "lifelike." In the context of a dream story, we expect things to happen as if we were dreaming. In the context of a mainstream novel about airports we expect wrenches to fall to the floor when they're released and a nervous mechanic to jump when the *ping!* comes off the concrete. In most stories, the reality we expect is more psychological than physical. We can accept ghosts passing through walls more readily than we accept a ghost who cannot love, hate, hunger, fear, take pleasure, feel envy, and so on. Usually even computers show emotion, or at least distress, in stories.

The only exception I can think of is the sentient ocean in Stanislaw Lem's novel *Solaris*. It attempts to communicate with humans by making physical their deepest thoughts. Unfortunately, those thoughts are usually nightmares and obsessions. The ocean keeps sending the main character's wife to visit him. She committed suicide in circumstances which make him feel very guilty. The emotional stress for the astronauts is horrible, but there is no indication the sentient ocean feels anything, though it might be argued that its trying to communicate with the "aliens" from Earth has a near-human dimension.

The realities we accept in stories cover a wide spectrum, but each story sets up rules the author has, by implication, promised the reader to follow. We do judge books by their covers and if we pick up a book that has a fabulously ripped man in a pirate shirt leaning over a buxom woman, we will be very irritated to discover a horror novel inside. The cover is the publisher's promise. The author's promise is in the choice of words, situation, and type of conflict presented in the first few pages and woe betide the author or publisher who breaks promises to the reader!

One promise that all authors make is to create a consistent reality. If there's magic in the novel's world, that's fine. If there isn't, that's fine, too. But you can't have it both ways and not make the reader feel that you are playing loose with your promises.

How does coincidence in the plot affect this? Coincidence makes for inconsistency. Let's say we have a novel in which a woman, Daisy Caramba, falls in love. She cannot live without Trueblood Ravenal and sets out to win him. She has some success, but suddenly Trueblood tells her she must forget him. He loves her but they must never see each other again. He tells Daisy nothing, but with a great effort Daisy cleverly discovers the truth. Trueblood is married! His wife is imprisoned for the murder of her mother and father! But Trueblood cannot divorce her under the laws of the Duchy of Gallstonia because all their mutual property is in her name. Fortunately, Trueblood's wife is stabbed to death by another inmate, so Daisy and Trueblood live happily ever after.

Huh? You say. What was that at the end? The wife gets shanked by an inmate? Whatta buncha crud! Whatever other problems this plot may have, this way of getting everything resolved is too cheap to contemplate. The author has not worked very hard to get the resolution to arise causally from what came before, and, by gum, we expect our authors to work hard!

Coincidence, like the *deus ex machina*, is an easy way out. By her preceding actions, Daisy has been set up as the kind of woman who works toward what she wants. To use the silly old adjective, she's "plucky." She went after Trueblood and she won his heart. In the (nearly insane) reality of this plot she is a person who is unrelenting. Her problem should be solved by what she does, not what is thrust into Trueblood's wife by an unknown prisoner. Daisy could fail in the end, or she could win, but in a satisfying plot, strange coincidences cannot take her off the hook.

Now it does no good to argue that exactly such a coincidence occurred with somebody you know or read about in the paper. As I said earlier, we are all aware that strange coincidences happen every day. The problem is that, no matter how realistic you intend to be, you are not creating the real world when you write, you are creating an artificial world. A story is not life, any more than the Venus de Milo is a woman. If life has a plot, the information's not available to the mortal man.

APPROPRIATE COINCIDENCES

But is there no role at all for coincidence in a plot? Yes, there is. If coincidence is a part of life, it can certainly be part of a plot. It's more of a question of how coincidence fits into the plot.

Where coincidence works most effectively is in the beginning. A whole chain of events might be precipitated by an interesting coincidence at the outset, and many novels begin this way without destroying the credibility of the plot. *The Day After Tomorrow*, Allan Folsom's bestselling thriller, begins with a doctor who is attending a conference in Paris. He's relaxing in a café when he recognizes the man who murdered his father many years before. The doctor was only a boy, but he cannot forget the killer, who was never identified or caught. This opening is marvelous. Even friends of mine who thought the novel as a whole was pretty silly told me that this was one of the best openings for a novel they had ever read. The fact that the beginning is an implausible coincidence doesn't harm the book at all.

A coincidence which begins the causal chain of a plot is more like the premise of the plot than an author's lazy way of working out the problem. What if a man who thought his mother died in a car wreck moved into the boarding house she now manages? What if the stock market crashes one day after a millionaire invests all her money? What if a boy finds a rare coin in his change on the day he runs away from an abusive father? All of these things are coincidental, but interesting plots could be developed from them. The coincidence at the beginning is little different from the other non-coincidental premises: a man thinks his mother died in a car accident, the stock market crashes, or the father is abusive. At the beginning of a plot we are willing to accept more because we are not yet involved in the linking of events. "There was an old woman who lived in a shoe." Okay, so what happened next?

So coincidence is okay at the beginning and bad at the ending. How does it work in the middle areas of the causal chain? That depends. As a general rule, the closer you are to the end, the less well it will work. After the beginning, any coincidence involves a risk. If any readers think it hard to believe in the coincidence, then you may lose them. It depends on how important the coincidence is to working out the plot. You are more likely to get away with small coincidences than larger ones. In André Gide's literary classic *The Counterfeiters*, a man is talking about counterfeit coins made of glass so that they ring like real coins. The listener pulls out exactly such a coin, drops it on the table, and says, "You mean like this?" Clearly it is a coincidence that he has one in his pocket, but it has no major impact on the plot itself, and therefore doesn't affect us that much.

I'll remind you that there are no absolute rules about how to write a novel, but, it is generally better to avoid all coincidences except those at the very beginning. If you do use one, use it carefully, and never as a means to resolve the primary conflict. Never let your readers think you're too lazy to work out the logic of your own plot.

BRAINSTORMER #3

Write a plot outline for your planned novel. This may take some time, but don't let it worry you. Consider the time an investment for the time you'll save later. Once it is finished subject it to a rigorous causal analysis. Go through the plot outline backwards. Become a child again and ask a series of "how – come's" until you get back to the beginning of the chain. Let's imagine doing this with the Trojan War plot I used earlier.

> Q: Why did Troy get burned?
> A: Because the Greeks tricked the Trojans with a wooden horse.
> Q: Why did the Greeks trick the Trojans?
> A: Because the war they were fighting seemed to be without end.
> Q: Why were they fighting the war then?
> A: Because Paris had run away with Helen.
> Q: So how come that would start a war?

And so on. This kind of meticulous checking will give you a greater understanding how your plot works and ought to reveal spots in your plot outline at which the connections are weak.

Would one event *necessarily* or *probably* be caused by the one preceding it? If it would not, or even iffy, then the causal link needs to be strengthened by altering the chain, the characters, or other elements.

Chapter 4
From Plot To Story

Let's begin this chapter by recalling that when the word "story" is used in this book, it refers to the entire presentation of plot, character, diction, thought, spectacle, and any other aspect of a story you wish to define, whether Aristotle's or not. I also use "story" as an all-inclusive term referring to the presentation within any narrative medium: novel, short story, film, epic poem, even jokes. The plot, however, is strictly the chronological structure underlying the story. Presenting a story is different from plotting it, and, as we have seen, because some people find plotting less fun than the other aspects of writing, they sometimes denigrate it.

It doesn't take a genius to notice that many stories (probably most) do not follow a strict chronological order, beginning at the beginning and following through to the conclusion. In fact, it was the advice of Aristotle, Horace, and many others to begin *in medias res*, "in the middle of things." This ancient technique for manipulating the plot can make the beginning of the story much more interesting than the beginning of a plot. Mighty oaks may indeed grow from tiny acorns, but a mighty oak is much more spectacular than an acorn. If we see the oak first, the acorn that begat it will take on new interest. You can't do too much to get the reader's attention these days. Hitting them between the eyes with an oak two-by-four is often necessary.

MAKING CONNECTIONS
When I served as the chairmen of a panel judging the Edgar Allan Poe award for the best "fact crime" book, I noticed the repeated use

of the *in medias res* technique in the nearly two hundred eligible non-fiction books. Each of the authors faced the problem of turning the circumstances around an actual crime into a book which would be as interesting as a novel and yet conform to what the author saw as the truth. Obviously, the way to make non-fiction as interesting as fiction is to use the techniques of plotting. However, the causal relationships among actual events is often unclear. Making those connections becomes a major problem for a non-fiction author who is telling a story. Ask any historian!

Serial killers were big the year I judged, and their lives usually provided the basic plot structure. Like Jack the Ripper, serial killers often increase the brutality of their crimes, thus providing a plot's rise in intensity. The causal chain for the plot would begin in childhood. In many cases, the killer was abused by one or both parents, foster parents, grandparents, step parents—you name them. After a series of such sickening experiences, the child grows up to become a very odd teenager. He experiments with more and more hideous cruelties, until he, too, becomes an abuser and then a demented killer. This theory of the serial killer's development may or may not be scientifically legitimate, but that's not the point.

The authors of these books often used the following story structure, rather than a chronological structure. The author would horrify the readers, getting their attention by showing the results of the killer's work. The opening chapter might consist of the serial killer getting ready to commit his most horrible crime. He has stalked his latest victim to her apartment house. The victim opens the door, and he rushes inside.

Usually the writers wouldn't give out the entire action of the killing at this point, but sometimes they would. The point, either way, was to slap the reader and say, "A woman died! Don't you want to know why?"

A common variation on this was to describe in great detail the grisly discovery of the body and the police inspection of the scene. The emphasis here was usually on the tracking of the killer, rather than his psychological development, though at some point when the suspect was identified, the book would usually jump back in time to where the killer grew up.

The story structure thus went like this:

1) The horrible crime by Jack Prevert at Chopping Lane.
2) Jack Prevert was born in Idabell, Oklahoma. His parents were dull.
3) Jack's parents died and he moved in with evil Granny Witch.
4) Granny Witch warps the lad.

And so on through Jack's life until we arrive back at the crime which opened the book. Putting the crime up front gives us a destination for our journey through this terrible person's life, which often was not much worse than the class president's. It allows the duller aspects of an ordinary life have future importance. If we were to read about a kid named Jack going to Idabell Elementary, without knowing he was going to become a maniacal killer, we might say, "What is the point of this? It isn't going anywhere."

So, then, it is obvious that a strict chronological plot may not be the best way to make a story entertaining. The technique of *in medias res* is used in both *The Iliad* and *The Odyssey*. When the former opens, we are well into the Trojan War and Achilles is already angry. When the latter opens, Odysseus is many years into his quest to return home and most of his adventures are told by him to others after he is cast up on their shores. *Hamlet* begins some time after the murder which the hero seeks to avenge. *The Tempest* begins after Prospero and his daughter have been stranded on their island for many years. Daphne Du Maurier's great opening line for *Rebecca*, "Last night I dreamt I went to Manderley again," places us in a reflective mode, well after the events of the novel, as do many novels which are "told" to us by a specific narrator. You could make a long list of murder mysteries which begin with the discovery of the body, but this is not the first event which begins the line of causes for the murder.

Mastering Plot

These are all uncovered later by the private eye or amateur detective and in many mysteries entire past scenes are recreated, rather than merely recounted to the detective.

Louis L'Amour once remarked that one of the most valuable things he had learned about writing came in his university study. He only spent a year at the University of Oklahoma, but he came under the tutelage of Walter Campbell, who wrote western books under the pen name of Stanley Vestal. To learn the craft of writing, Campbell got L'Amour to read various great writers, but particularly the French writer Balzac. What young L'Amour learned, he said, was very simple and led him to becoming one of the most successful writers in the world. Find the beginning, and start *after* that. It has worked for thousands of years and will work for you, too.

THE FLASHBACK

When scenes from the past interrupt the chronological flow of a story, we call these a "flashback," and beginning writers often find them to be an irresistible decoration. It seems like *real writing* needs to have flashbacks and I'd like a nickel for every student who has asked me if their manuscripts needed flashbacks. No manuscript *needs* a flashback. Many novels get along fine without them. The question is: does the flashback contribute to advancing the plot or adding depth in a significant way? Think of a flashback like a musical number in a Broadway play. It shouldn't be there merely to pretty up the show. It should also take the plot to a higher level, building intensity like any other scene.

Let's try an example. Gretchen Hoopskirt is a aging schoolmarm in the Old West. She is in the General Store buying asafetida for her bronchitis when a man walks in. He hardly notices her. They nod politely to each other. Gretchen leaves, but waits outside as the man climbs into a buggy chatting with two other men. She watches them leave, her heart pounding, wondering if he recognized her. Now we go into the flashback. Gretchen is sixteen and living in St. Joseph when a boy, Dick Dastardly, approaches her. He is exciting and daring and teaches her more than just how to make love. They burglarize a hotel's pantry at four in the morning. A night watchman catches Dick. Gretchen in a panic cracks the man over the head with a frying pan. He drops, dead as the proverbial doornail.

The flashback ends as Gretchen remembers they ran away together, and Dick deserted her within a month. The only thing she knows about Dick is that he became an infamous, murderous bank robber. What if Dick is here to steal and possibly murder? How can she warn the good sheriff? No one ever knew about the dead night watchman but Dick. Exposing Dick Dastardly might put a noose around her own neck!

The chronology of this episode would go from Gretchen's meeting Dick years ago to their coincidental encounter in the store. And telling the story in that order wouldn't be wrong. Oftentimes the best way to tell a story is also the simplest way, but writers can get so wrapped up in admiring techniques that they try to make their stories more complicated. Complicating a story unnecessarily won't make an uninteresting story more interesting, just more difficult. The techniques may keep the reader from creating the emotion essential to making the story compelling. You've got to trust the underlying story.

However, if we tell Gretchen's story the way it is represented above, we might gain by the flashback. First, there will be a period (albeit short) in which the reader is wondering why the schoolmarm is behaving so peculiarly. Who is this stranger? Why does his presence disturb her? By the end of the flashback we will have discovered our initial impression of Gretchen is deeper than we thought. If we already knew Gretchen's past, some of the voltage might be taken from the encounter in the store.

Our reaction to Gretchen will be different. Will the reader first come to know her as an upright schoolmarm or as a misled teenager? As the schoolmarm we are more likely to want to root for her and think of the killing as an accident. As the teenager we might be more inclined to think that she should have been smart enough to stay away from Dick, that murder will out, and that fate is finally bringing her what she deserves.

Another aspect of this is that the main body of the story deals with the conflict between schoolmarm Gretchen and the mature Dick Dastardly. The story problem begins not with the hotel burglary but with Dick's turning up in the new life she has built. By using the flashback we can begin our story at the crucial moment in the schoolmarm's life..

As all flashbacks should do, this one significantly changes the meaning of what's going on. It not only adds more information, but it more spectacularly reveals why Gretchen's problem is larger than it appears. In the best flashbacks, the revelation of what happened becomes a way to comment on what is happening in the story's "present." In pointless flashbacks, the material from the past only confirms what we already know. The direction of the story doesn't change because of the flashback. If a flashback does nothing but pad the information, it probably shouldn't be there.

Suppose, for example, the situation's the same but when Gretchen recognizes the stranger it is because she once saw him loading crates in a wagon in St. Louis and berating his son for not helping adequately. There was no hotel burglary. Gretchen perhaps thinks of him as a cad, but it doesn't change her behavior, create a problem, clarify something odd, or in any other way alter the course of the plot. Why would we devote a scene merely to demonstrating that a man who walked into a store is mean to his children? It might be possible if it had great impact on something later in the plot, but as it stands it doesn't.

With flashbacks you also risk disorienting your reader. Not handled carefully, readers can get confused about what happened when. In a straight chronological narrative there is little risk of this, of course. One thing follows another. In a story which uses what is called a "frame story" (which we'll discuss in more detail later), there is also little risk because in its simplest form only two transitions are required. In the time which begins the story, someone tells a story which took place in the past. We jump back to it. At the end of the story in the past, we move back to the storyteller.

Although many stories employ flashbacks and other shifts through time to create effects, you should not automatically assume that a story *needs* a flashback or a frame story.

Simpler is better ninety-nine percent of the time. Look at all your favorite novels and short stories and you will see that even those which use flashbacks, flashforwards, frame stories, or both, most tell the story in large chunks which are in chronological order.

The best stories have nothing irrelevant in them. Don't use flashbacks in your story without a compelling reason.

THE FLASH FORWARD

Flash forwards are similar to flashbacks, but are less commonly used. They appear when an author departs from the present of the main story and jumps into the future. For example, in Laura Ingalls Wilder's *Little House in the Big Woods*, she writes of waking one morning in the fall to see a deer hanging in the tree out front. The venison is delicious and Laura wishes they could eat it all, but most of the meat must be salted and packed away for winter.

> Soon the snow would come. Then the log house would be almost buried in snowdrifts, and the lakes and the streams would freeze....The bears would be hidden away in their dens....The rabbits would be shy and swift....Pa might hunt alone all day in the bitter cold...and come home with nothing for Ma and Mary and Laura to eat.

The scene then shifts back to the fall and the Ingalls family preparing for winter.

As in Wilder's book, the flashforward is used as a way of informing what is going on in the present. If she had simply gone on with the salting and storing, its urgency would not have been established as well as it was by this vision of the animals and the winter in the Big Woods.

An appropriate flashforward adds greater meaning to the ground situation of the story. I have often noticed the use of it in stories dealing with childhood. The adult narrator interrupts with an insight on how a childish thing may lead to adult consequences, but since the story is about the child and not the adult, the author flashes forward, then back to the original narrative. We might see a young girl discover that her mother is unfaithful. Though she cannot understand this as a child, she grows up to understand what she discovered when she came home early from school. The author might then flash forward to a scene which reveals the woman's inability to maintain a successful marriage before returning to the story of the girl. If done right, the flashforward will establish the importance of the moment that the girl could not grasp.

A flashforward can add a sense of irony or tragic inevitability in certain contexts. It might show that these happy moments we are reading about will lead to disaster, or that the girl and boy which despise each other in junior high school end up being the only couple in their neighborhood that hasn't been divorced.

A fascinating use of flashforwards appears in the Nicholas Roeg film *Don't Look Now.* In it a man continually has strange visions which disturb him. He seems to be psychically picking up images from a murder which has taken place in the past. At the end of the film, however, we discover that each of these visions is actually a flashforward. The man is having visions of his own murder. The film makes you think the flashforwards are flashbacks and provides a shocking climax.

Flashforwards can be useful, but overused they can be very tedious. A flashforward should not usually give away the climax of the main storyline. If it does, it will take away from the tension. The exception to this is when you are invoking inevitability. The flashforward in these cases is set in a future somewhat remote from the "present." It is not really the climax of the main story, but a result of the climax. Then, at least your reader can wonder how such a thing could come about. It works like a foreshadowing opening line.

The greatest such line is probably the one that begins Gabriel García Márquez's *One Hundred Years of Solitude*: "Many years later, as he faced the firing squad, Colonel Aureliano Buendía was to remember that distant afternoon when his father took him to discover ice." We begin in a difficult situation in the future, but it takes many pages before we get the Colonel back in front of the firing squad. We are intrigued by the sentence, but it doesn't kill our interest because the progress from the ice to the firing squad hasn't been given away. The remark about the firing squad also adds special meaning to his memory of the traveling carnival with its display of ice.

FRAME STORIES

A moment ago we mentioned the frame story, which is another variation on the simplest form of a plot. It's not a very complicated device and is similar to a flashforward, though you experience it *before* the main story, rather than *during*. A frame story brackets or "frames" the main story, setting up the premise that the main story is being told or written some time after it took place. A simple frame story might run as follows:

> A man sat by a campfire and this is the story he told. "In the town I grew up in, there was an old woman who lived in a shoe…"

At the end of the story we might have:

> "…then she whipped them soundly and sent them to bed." The man leaned back, stretched his hands toward the fire and lit his pipe.

Like bookends, the two parts of the man telling the story sit on the ends of the main story constituting the frame within which the story is told. There are many examples of this structuring in literature. How about the beginning of Mark Twain's *A Connecticut Yankee in King Arthur's Court*?

Mastering Plot

> It was in Warwick Castle that I came across the curious stranger whom I am going to talk about. He attracted me by three things: his candid simplicity, his marvelous familiarity with ancient armor, and the restfulness of his company — for he did all the talking. We fell together, as modest people will, in the tail of the herd that was being shown through, and he at once began to say things which interested me. As he talked along, softly, pleasantly, flowingly, he seemed to drift away imperceptibly out of this world and time, and into some remote era and old forgotten country; and so he gradually wove such a spell about me that I seemed to move among the specters and shadows and dust and mold of a gray antiquity, holding speech with a relic of it!

In this way, Twain moves into his fantastical story about a man transported through time.

The frame story usually takes up much less space than the main body of a novel because it usually isn't as important as the central struggle. But, if it isn't as important, why have it at all? Again, beginning writers are often tempted by the technique of the frame story when it isn't necessary. The properly functioning and effective frame story changes the meaning of the story it frames.

One critic remarked that every first-person story (like *Moby Dick* or *The Great Gatsby*) is really about the effect of the story on the narrator. Thus Ishmael's changed perception of the universe is the real subject of *Moby Dick*, not the more colorful Captain Ahab, and the effect of Gatsby on Nick Carraway is the subject of *The Great Gatsby*, not Jay Gatsby himself. We are always aware in reading a book narrated by "I" of that character's traits. We are never entirely sure we can trust that what the character is saying is what really happened.

Not all frame stories employ an I-narrator, but all of them create a similar psychic distance from the central story. This can help a story work well or it can hurt it. People often forget that Henry James's novella *The Turn of the Screw* has a frame story. The powerful central conflict involves two frightened children under the control of a governess who is either imagining that ghosts are out to get them, or who is not imagining and the ghosts *are* out to get them. The fact that this central story has a frame story in which one man tells another the story of the governess adds a number of interesting dimensions to the entire work. If we were to take the story as merely a ghost story, it might lose a lot of its psychological dimension. We would merely accept it as a ghost story or not accept it. Why is this story significant to the man who is telling it? Could it be, as one critic suggested, that the man is actually the boy in the story many years later, still trying to deal with the trauma? The distance created by this way of telling the story allows us to find a possible deeper meaning in it.

There are frames around many stories which we might find more difficulty in accepting if there was none, such as in *Turn of the Screw* and *A Connecticut Yankee*. Apparently, setting up the situation in which someone is explaining a story they heard allows us to suspend more easily our normal disbelief of the bizarre. Notice how in those urban folk tales which circulate, there is usually a mini-frame story. "A friend of my cousin's went to school with a girl who never washed her beehive hairdo. She dropped dead one day and it was discovered that spiders had nested in her hairdo and drilled into her brain. I'm telling you that's what I heard anyway."

The friend of a friend provides distance that allows the teller of the story to be as surprised as the listener. The teller can imply she wouldn't believe it either, if it hadn't come from a friend of a friend, and the listener can identify with the teller. At the same time there is an illusion of verification. The story would not be as credible if the teller had "heard somewhere once" about a girl with a spider nest in her do. The device of the frame makes it more credible and folk tales like this spread from coast to coast.

Another frame that people often overlook in famous writing is the one in Shakespeare's *Taming of the Shrew*. The script itself begins with a trick being played upon a character named Christopher Sly. He's drunk as a lord, and passes out, so several of his friends take it upon themselves to make him think he *is* a lord who has been dreaming he's the sot Christopher Sly. During this deception, they offer Sly a play, which is the story of a froward shrew, Kate, tamed by a spirited man named Petruchio.

Productions of Shakespeare's play often dump the Sly business. It isn't all that funny and doesn't seem all that related to the main story. Furthermore, in the existing texts of *Taming of the Shrew*, Christopher Sly never returns to close the frame at the end. If you think about it, however, the Sly frame is sly indeed. It makes the tale of Petruchio and Kate into a fairy tale. It becomes a "let's suppose." It prevents it from being taken as a true story. Therefore, when Petruchio's rough treatment of Kate seems distasteful or offensive, we can laugh, as if we're watching slapstick: Moe cracks Larry and Curly over the head, or the Wile E. Coyote tumbles into a canyon. We know it's just a story. When the amazing conversion of Kate to the best wife in Christendom occurs, it is far too tidy an ending, but we can temporarily accept it the same way we accept, "And they lived happily ever after."

Historians tell us there was much controversy in Shakespeare's time about the proper status of women. Some argued that women were in all ways equal to men; others found scriptural "proof" that women, like cats and ferns, had no souls—though this could be a difficult argument with Elizabeth I on the throne. Most of society probably fell somewhere in between these views. Putting the frame on the story of the shrew allows it to be humorously distanced—less serious and less touchy.

In our own time, *The Taming of the Shrew* seems so remote, that there is little need to distance it. Actors do their thigh-slapping Petruchios and their snarling Kates in an overdone way that distances it even more. Take a look at the Richard Burton and Elizabeth Taylor film of the play directed by Franco Zefirrelli. There's a kind of winking at the audience: har! har! We don't really mean this, folks! In a novel, the equivalent winking could come from the tone of the prose: "Once upon a time in a kingdom far away, there lived a froward shrew."

In a BBC production of *Taming of the Shrew* which starred John Cleese and was directed by Jonathan Miller, you got quite a different effect. Cleese played Petruchio with a sincerity not usually present in productions of it, undermining the distancing effected by the frame story, but producing a more thought-provoking and credible version. Maybe it's less true to the spirit of Shakespeare and maybe it is *more* true. We cannot know. In a prose version the equivalent tone would be more like this: "In May of 1504, a young man named Petruchio rode into Padua on a seedy roan. He was looking for a wife and a large dowry was his object."

But you are not writing *The Taming of the Shrew.* Should you structure your story within a frame? Consider some of the factors discussed above. Remember: the best stories have nothing irrelevant in them. Do not use a frame story without a purpose.

OUTLINING YOUR STORY

"Oh, no," you gasp, "you're not going to tell me to do another outline!" I know. The plot outline was hard enough, but quit complaining. The bulk of the work is done, if you've done your plot outline properly. You've established the chain of cause and effect. You have a clearer idea of what central problem or conflict serves as the engine for the entire novel. You have a good sense of what begins the conflict and what ends it.

What you're going to do with your plot now is become more inventive with the structure in order to make it more interesting to read. Instead of a stodgy rectangular frame house, you might try the structure of an A-frame chalet or a geodesic dome. You don't want to be so clever you ruin your novel with a bizarre structure. On the other hand, a few alterations might make what was routine become more interesting.

First, as we discussed earlier, look for an interesting place for your novel to begin. Consider the ancient advice of Aristotle and Horace and look for the possibility of beginning *in medias res.* Consider what Louis L'Amour said was his lifelong principle: to find the beginning and start the novel after that. Is there a scene with drama and emotion that gives the flavor of the novel but isn't so far into the chain of events that you would have to spend long sections recovering what happened before?

I recently received a student outline for a fantasy novel. It was to have a prologue in which the fantasy kingdom and the coming of the evil wizard's legions was to be described. In the first chapter following the prologue, the queen would desperately be trying to spirit her baby daughter away from the evil wizard's army. It was easy to see that the book would begin much more effectively at the first chapter.

She saw that by beginning when the evil wizard began his war of conquest was a great deal less interesting than by beginning at the moment in which the evil wizard's legions are coming over the walls. Fire! Blood! Screaming! The queen running through corridors with the baby wrapped in a blanket! What will they do?

The rest of the book would concern itself with this baby's growing to be a warrior princess who would overturn the reign of the evil wizard. Scanning the outline the writer could see the primary struggle would be between the warrior princess and the wizard. How the wizard came to rule was previous to the stability of his ruling, which would be overturned by the princess. The writer wisely dumped her prologue. Whatever information was in it could be recapitulated within the novel later.

Second, consider how reordering some of the chronology might help to make your intentions clearer. This is similar to beginning *in medias res*, except that (as in our previous example) individual scenes will diverge from the chronology. Let me explain it this way. If we think of a plot as a line running from A, an earlier point in time, through B to F, a later point in time, it will look like this:

$$A----B----C----D----E----F$$

This example is overly simple, being a story with only six scenes, but it will make the point. In many cases this kind of straightforward, simple plot will work fine. Begin and go straight to the ending. Why not?

If we begin *in medias res*, however, we will break the straight time line. So that we have something like this:

$$C----D----E----F$$

In this latter scheme the details of A and B will be revealed in passing through the others, or perhaps in D a character tells the story of A and B, but they will not necessarily be set up in separate scenes. Basically, the chronology of events is in the same order.

However, flashbacks might create schemes like these:

$$C----A----D----B----E----F$$

or

$$C----D----E----F----A----B$$

In the first of these two, the flashbacks inform what is happening in the C through F plot. In the second, the flashback serves as a climax, explaining what C through F was all about, as in one of those psychiatry stories in which the trauma which afflicts the patient must be explained.

And, of course, there is the simple flashback, in which most of the story is chronological, except for an occasional flashback. In this scheme of six, there is only one:

$$B----C----A----D----E----F$$

A frame story might be diagramed in the following way:

$$F1----A----B----C----D----E----F2$$

F happens after A through E, but is split to enclose the main story.

Now, if I were a better mathematician, I could tell you how many possible arrangements could be made of our six letters (or theoretical plot events). Suffice it to say, a whole lot. Especially if we allow splitting, as we did in our frame story. So consider how many arrangements might be made of a theoretical dramatic movie script, which consists of approximately thirty scenes and who knows how many plot events. A scene usually contains at least one plot event and often more than one. And novels are often much more complex than movies. Some arrangements of the events, maybe most of them, wouldn't work at all in a coherent story, but that will still leave many choices to the writer.

I am reminded of Julio Cortazar's experimental novel *Rayuela* (translated as *Hopscotch*). In it there are 155 chapters. The reader is told, however, that the book can be read from chapter one to chapter 59, where the first version of the book ends. The reader can also read it in the order of a list provided, which begins with chapter 74, goes to 1, 2, 116, 3, 84, 4, 71 and so on. Read as 1 through 59, you have one impression of the novel. Read in a different order, you have another. Really, *Hopscotch* is a huge and elaborate parlor trick. The quality of the writing in Spanish makes it more significant than the usual parlor trick, but it isn't the kind of novel you'd want to use as a model. However, it does make an important point. The order of scenes determines the nature of the novel.

WARNING! SIMPLE IS GOOD

Once again, however, let me speak for simplicity. Rearranging the plot merely for the sake of making it more writerly almost always makes it less effective. Readers don't want a puzzle they have to sort out. They don't want to be confused about what's going on. Never forget that.

Oh, yes, you can hold back things as teasers. Why is this man crying while he picks up a new car? In the flashback we find out that it is because his father's only wish in life was to drive a new car and the man died before it could happen. What the writer must not allow to happen is confusion over whether the father died before his son picks up the car, or confusion about whether the son is picking up a car, or confusion about whether the son is twelve or thirty years old.

Such confusions seem incredible, but do happen when writers try to be too clever.

Don't play tricks on the reader. Never get so "artistic" that you bewilder them. That is the *least* artistic thing you can do.

When you have created a plot outline, it is much easier to consider how these kinds of rearrangements might make your story more exciting.

BRAINSTORMER #4

Let's borrow a technique that is common among screenwriters, but that I and many other novelists have used with complicated stories. Screen writers make index cards of each scene and tack them up in order on a cork board. This is such a useful method that the best screenwriting softwares include a way to do "cards" on the screen. The cards give them an overview of their entire film, just as your plot outline gives you an overview of your plot. They can then rearrange cards, throw cards out, and add cards to make their story more effective. When it seems right for what they want to do with their script, they write it.

You can do a similar thing with index cards, or any other way you find effective. Word processors cut and paste easily, though it is hard to see the full outline at once. Take the plot outline you created in the previous chapter and briefly summarize each step in the causal chain on index cards. If you're feeling artsy-craftsy you could cut out each step and stick it to a card. It doesn't matter. Playing is good for you. Just don't eat the paste.

Initially, arrange these cards in the original chronological order. Tack them to a cork board, but you can stick them on the wall or spread them on a table or whatever.

First, consider how changing the order of these cards might affect your novel. All of the principles explained in this chapter are to be applied. Try beginning *in medias res*, for example, or inverting the order of scenes. Move some of the events earlier in the chronology into flashback positions. Look at it, think about it. Consider throwing out weak scenes. Consider the worth of a frame story. Consider combining two scenes into one and if it works, make a new card to replace the other two. Rearrange the cards until you are satisfied with the way your story is presented. Once you have rearranged your plot outline into a more effective sequence of events, you have a story outline for your novel.

Soon you will begin the really hard work: writing it well.

Chapter 5
The Beginning

Now that you have drawn up a story outline and carefully checked to see that your plot is based on a clear causal chain of events, you will need to address the problem of magnitude, which I briefly discussed in the previous chapter. Aristotle's remarks about magnitude are very common-sensical as he says that the beauty of an object is a combination of its order and magnitude. If an animal is too small to be perceived, regardless how well-arranged its parts are, its beauty cannot be experienced. Diatoms, plankton, pollen, and even dust mites can be beautiful when enlarged by microphotography to a magnitude at which we can see and appreciate their parts. If, on the other hand, a creature is too large, it cannot be experienced as a whole.

Aristotle asks us to imagine a thousand-mile-long animal, and I'm reminded of the old Indian story of the blind men and the elephant. One grabs the elephant's tail and says the elephant is like a snake. Another grabs the elephant's leg and says it is like a tree. Another touches the ear and says it is like a giant leaf. I'm also reminded of the remark that the environmental movement got its greatest boost when the astronauts returned with their photos of the earth from space. Suddenly, it is said, people could grasp the conception of the earth as a blue marble, a fragile island in the hostile darkness of space. There it was—the entire earth. Clouds and oceans and continents: all of it in a magnitude we could now experience.

So, then, of what magnitude should a plot be? Aristotle says that a plot-structure should be of a length which can easily be held in the

Mastering Plot

memory. That makes good sense. If we could not remember how a plot began, we wouldn't be able to enjoy where it was going.

Ray Bradbury wrote a short story in which time travelers hunt dinosaurs. They have walkways to make certain they do not alter the future accidentally. (As if plugging dinosaurs with shotguns wouldn't change anything! But let that go for the moment). One of the hunters steps off the path, crushing a flower. When the hunters return to the present, all of history has been altered and the Nazis won World War II. Now, if we are to accept this story's logic, we must accept that the crushing of the flower somehow causes the Nazis to win. One event causes the next, in some mysterious way. In a leap of faith, the readers jump over the intervening millions of years.

Try to imagine, however, that Bradbury had tried to work out all the connections within that leap. When the flower was crushed it did not produce seed and this seed was the last chance for a particular colony of ants to survive which had a mutation which allowed ants to…. You get the idea. No matter how clever all these connections are, the sheer number and size of them over the time period would be impossible to hold in the mind.

The appropriate magnitude of a plot, however, cannot easily be defined. You've undoubtedly seen many motion pictures based upon books. Often if the book is a large, complex one, its magnitude is not suitable to be jammed into the two hours of a movie. *Bonfire of the Vanities* by Tom Wolfe is quite easy to grasp when read, but it has many things going on in its wide-angle picture of New York City. When it was adapted for film, it seemed confused and disorderly. There are many adaptation of monster novels like *War and Peace*, *Les Miserables,* or *Nicholas Nickleby*, or Stephen King's *The Stand*, but these novels are so large that film makers must cut out huge swaths of their stories. The John Huston adaptation of *Moby Dick* is a memorable fine effort, but contains only a fraction of the original. *Lord of the Rings* was made into four long films. Television miniseries and binge watching has made some such endurable for the screen, but large chunks must still be removed for visual media.

Appropriate magnitude then varies according to the medium. It also varies according to the genre. Mystery, western, and romance novels, for example, tend to have less complicated plots, though they may be highly complex books as to character, psychology, and social insight. Literary novels vary from hugely complex plots to tiny ones which microscopically examine character or emotional events. It isn't easy to say what magnitude of a plot fits which medium. Many of us discover this by trial and error. We write a short story that gets well beyond the reasonably publishable length of 2500 to 4500 words, and don't have any idea what to do with it. Or we think we has this great idea for a novel and yet it isn't sufficient to fill two hundred pages. Just sticking in more stuff—say, more events and characters—only pads it and makes it dull. It is an idea that is perfect at an awkward length. All you can do is hope to find a publisher interested in works of unusual size, or perhaps include it in a booklength collection.

THE REVERSAL OF FORTUNE

Another way of looking at the problem of magnitude can help. Aristotle refuses to be specific about the appropriate length of a drama or an epic poem, but says that it should be the size required for a probable and necessary chain of events which effects a transformation from happiness to misery, or to the reverse. In other words, we might say that an appropriate length for a plot is the length that is required for a series of events to bring about a reversal of fortune. A story is about change and how it comes about in one particular case.

From misery to happiness or the reverse might seem a bit narrow in our times, but the general principle applies. We could say that most romances are about moving from loveless misery to eternal marital happiness. Plots in which the good guy takes on the bad guy and wins, can also be said to move from misery to happiness. But there are other emotions than misery and happiness. The common novel of growing up (a. k. a. the *Bildungsroman* when we're feeling pompous) is about the main character's passage from immaturity to maturity, as in *The Red Badge of Courage*. Henry might be said to be moving from a kind of misery to a kind of happiness, but it matters more that he changes. He becomes more self-aware. There are many novels in which a complacently unaware person has a shattering experience which forces them into self-awareness. The novel, *Hannibal*, does this with both Clarice Starling and Hannibal Lector. So does Tom Wolfe's *A Man in Full* although his main character, Charlie Croker, is nothing like anyone in the Harris novel.

Plots are a struggle in which change occurs. Change doesn't come easy. Why would a person change if not forced to? Therefore, the chain of events is usually precipitated by a cataclysm of some kind. There is a stable situation which turns unstable, and the protagonist struggles to make life stable again. I might add here that a stable situation isn't very interesting, which is why stories are about disorder.

In the novel *Atticus* by Ron Hansen, Atticus is a tough old farmer whose son lives in Mexico. He receives word that his son has committed suicide. He cannot believe it and goes to Mexico to recover the body and eventually to be confirmed in his belief that his son was murdered. Through this agony he comes to appreciate his son in a different way. In *A Man in Full*, Charlie Croker is a wealthy real estate developer whose empire falls apart when his loans default. He cannot imagine life without all his expensive comforts. Ironically, he comes to accept losing all his possessions and weirdly proselytizes for Stoicism. Sam Spade begins *The Maltese Falcon* as what Hammett describes as a "blond Satan." He cheats with his partner's wife. He seems to have few ethics. But when Brigid O'Shaughnessy comes into his life, he falls in love despite himself. He must deal with that as well as his conflicting obligation to do right by his murdered partner.

A plot puts someone under pressure and keeps him or her under pressure. The pressure cooker is the only way to change them in any significant way, and in a worthwhile plot there is always a movement toward change. You might object that some series characters don't change very much. Often in series novels the characters undergoing change are more the secondary characters than the protagonist. Miss Marple is Miss Marple in Agatha Christie's novels and Jack Reacher is Jack Reacher in the novels of Lee Child. However, there is a stable situation (say for Miss Marple, it's life in St. Mary Mead). In mysteries it is usually a murder that destabilizes the situation. The solving of the murder returns things to their original state, or almost. Quite often even in such series, however, you will notice subtle changes in the character. Even Sherlock Holmes develops slightly through his stories. Many repeating characters get older. At one time mystery writer Dorothey Sayers was considered a much more literary writer in her genre because she developed the relationship between her characters Lord Peter Wimsey and Harriet Vane. Currently, the trend in publishing is clearly towards the main character undergoing change, as publishers have cancelled such repetitious series as that long-running older one featuring Mack Bolan, the Executioner. Entertainment in which the hero is always the same age, with remarkably little memory for anything he or she has undergone is for simpler media. Publishers now pretty much leave such repetitiousness to television.

If we look at the plotting of television series (with the exceptions of shows like *Hill Street Blues* or *Breaking Bad* or the series on HBO, Showtime, and the like), the goal is to end an episode about where it began. We see a movement from stability to instability to stability. Does the following sound like an episode of the old series *Happy Days*? Richie and Potsie are friends. They both date the same girl. They argue and fight. Fonzi, however, intervenes and they come to see that friendship is more important. The episode ends in reconciliation. Maybe it's not a great plot and it delivers no great insight, but you know what? Our imaginary *Happy Days* plot is very similar to Shakespeare's *Two Gentlemen of Verona*. The plot is not the problem.

STARTING WITH THE PROBLEM

If we look at a plot as a movement from stability to instability to stability, the beginning is the moment at which instability is introduced. Instability introduces a period of struggle to re-establish stability, though that ending stability may be quite different from the initial stability. One of the best examples of a play going straight for the throat is Aristotle's favorite, *Oedipus the King* by Sophocles. The stable situation is that Oedipus is king of Thebes, and married to Jocasta. In the very first scene, the people of Thebes come to him and explain that a terrible curse is upon the land. Crops are failing, people are hungry, and so on. That, obviously, is the instability which Oedipus as a good king must struggle to end. He does not know that it will lead to his own destruction. By play's end he will have discovered that he himself is the source of the curse, that he killed his father and married his mother. Jocasta will commit suicide and Oedipus will gouge out his own eyes at the sight of her body. At the end, he will be led offstage by a little boy to wander the earth as a beggar, but he will have re-established the stability of his kingdom through his own suffering.

You might object that Thebes has not really been re-stabilized, because subsequent myths, dramatized in plays like Sophocles' *Antigone* and Aeschylus' *Seven Against Thebes*, show much disorder in the kingdom. However, these disorders, though related, are not the direct result of Oedipus' actions. *Oedipus the King* is about the single "action" (as Aristotle calls it) of Oedipus' struggle to remove the curse he has inadvertently imposed on his people.

Summarized, the story of Oedipus sounds insane, but as Sophocles wrote it, it is one of the most powerful statements of the human condition ever made. If you've read it, you know just how rapidly the struggle begins. As I mentioned earlier, Oedipus appears on stage with the chorus (the people of Thebes) before him, weeping and lamenting. The first line of the play is his question: "Oh my children, the new blood of ancient Thebes, why are you here?" Bang! We're off! The conflict has begun. It isn't always easy to find the precise moment to begin a plot, but old Sophocles—he lived to ninety!—knew a thing or two. We cannot do better than to learn from the old man who is still read after two thousand years.

Aristotle, when he writes of the genius of Homer, points out that *The Iliad* is but a sliver of the Trojan War. It begins with the poet saying (in Robert Fagles' translation), "Rage—goddess, sing the wrath of Peleus' son Achilles." Again the moment of the commencement of instability begins the great poem. Agamemnon has taken a slave girl that Achilles thinks by right of looting ought to belong to him, When Achilles gets angry, he refuses to fight. This turns the tide of war so drastically, that the Greeks are nearly driven into the sea. After all these years of keeping the Trojans at bay (the dreadful stability of a stalemated war), the Greeks are going to be defeated. A desperate attempt by Achilles' friend Patroclus to save the Greeks ends with Patroclus' death at the hands of Hector. Achilles emerges from his sulk in a brutal rage and fights Hector, *mano a mano*, killing him. When Achilles' rage finally subsides (as he gives Hector's mutilated body to Hector's father), the story is over. Never mind how many more years remain in the Trojan War. The stability of the nearly pointless ten-year struggle has returned and *The Iliad* ends with the situation much as it was at the beginning when Achilles' anger destabilized it.

Consider the openings of other famous stories. *Hamlet* begins with soldiers talking about the strange appearance of a ghost. The ghost, Prince Hamlet's father, destabilizes the situation. Something is rotten in the state of Denmark, and it must be cleaned out. The ghost will set Prince Hamlet on a quest to determine the facts in his father's death. After a long struggle, stability will return because of Hamlet's revenge on his uncle and the invasion of Fortinbras, who takes over the kingdom in the last scene.

Keep in mind, too, that a form of instability or disorder might be what constitutes the initial stability.

Huh? you say. Imagine the following plot. A city is in chaos. There is no law and order, and gangs abuse all the inhabitants. The Martians land and immediately impose an authoritarian regime in which the gangs are eliminated and disorder is utterly rooted out. Humans, however, find this order stifling. To paraphrase Harry Lime's remark in *The Third Man*, all this law and order is only producing cuckoo clocks. Humankind is bored. It revolts and after a great struggle overcomes the Martians. People then immediately return to the gang warfare that began our plot, as miserable as they were at the outset. So, then, in terms of the lives of our characters, the story moved from instability to stability to instability. However, in story terms, the initial chaos or instability *is* the stability.

As with plays, effective movies begin fast, getting to the central problem as quickly as possible. There may be a few initial moments to establish the stable situation that is to be destabilized, but that is done quickly. It's the struggle that's interesting. In *Men Don't Leave*, starring Jessica Lange, a happy family is shattered by the father's sudden death and must completely change its lifestyle by moving to the city. In *The Seven Samurai*, Akira Kurosawa's great film, a village which is being victimized by bandits sends a man to find "out-of-work" samurai to protect it. *There's Something About Mary* begins with the protagonist meeting the girl of his dreams, as does *Life is Beautiful* (*La Vita è Bella*), two very different comedies.

The same general rule follows with novels. Again, there may be several scenes setting up the stable situation that is to be destroyed, but an effective author gets to the struggle as quickly as possible, often in the first line. Herman Melville's *Moby Dick* begins with Ishmael's depression, which he feels can only be cured by a sea voyage. *Farewell, My Lovely* is set in motion by Moose Malloy's request that Philip Marlowe find Velma Grayle. *Lolita* begins with Humbert Humbert's chant of desire for the underage girl of the title which he will spend the novel trying to keep for his own. Stephen King's *Bag of Bones* begins with the death of author Michael Noonan's wife, leading to Noonan's inability to write.

In any plotline, if the writer does not know what the central problem is, the moment at which the problem begins will be obscure, as well as when ending has occurred. The reader will take away only a vague sense of why the events happened, or will feel no sense of resolution at the end. In many plots the central problem seems obvious. The murder takes place, the murderer is unmasked by the detective. These events are like two brackets holding the plot in between them. Girl meets boy, they fall into each others' arms. Hostile Martians come to earth, they are defeated. Bad guys ride into a cow town and terrorize it, the marshal wipes out the gangs in a gunfight. It isn't always this easy, however, to summarize the core problem.

Many beginning writers are not certain precisely what the central problem of their novel is. They know, for example, that it is about a woman trying to find herself when her husband deserts her, but they are vague about what that means. Is the main character a deep believer in marriage and therefore has to learn to adjust to a world in which a marriage may be tossed aside? Or is she intent on replacing one marriage with another, so that her struggle is to find another husband? Could her problem be primarily economic: the loss of her husband forces her to become a breadwinner? Or is the primary struggle about coming to some realization about herself and her feelings about men, perhaps her relationship with her abusive father and the way she chooses men who are similarly abusive? The fact that her husband leaves her may well begin the struggle, but what is the struggle about?

Outlining the plot can be useful in solving this problem because it allows you to get an overall view of the entire plot. Many beginning novelists spend a lot of time in their first chapter trying to describe the main character, rather than throwing the character into a frying pan. Often this takes the form of a character's waking up, roaming around the house, and thinking about what is in store for today. This usually isn't very interesting unless something is immediately injected into the opening.

A fairly common device is that the telephone may ring with some sort of news that gets things moving. I used this trick in my second novel, *White Rook*. The phone awakens detective Dub Greenert, who looks around at the shabbiness of his life as he is offered an investigation into a possible murder. The shabby stability of his life is altered by that phone call and the central problem of the investigation into an ultra-right wing paramilitary group begins.

But, even though I use my own novel as an example, I don't recommend waking up the main character as a beginning. There are no absolute rules about writing, other than "Be interesting." If you can make a character waking up interesting and exciting, by all means write it. However, having something dynamic going on in your initial scene is a better way to be interesting, as long as it is combined with the initiation of instability. A crowd comes to the palace of King Oedipus to solicit his help. A man comes into a police station and dies on the floor. A woman enters a rest home to visit her father and discovers he has wandered off. At the beginning of your plot, the characterization is less important than getting the reader engaged in a problem. The working out of the problem will give you the opportunity to reveal all you want about your character.

Take *Oedipus the King* again. When the play begins, we have no idea of Oedipus' character. He is a king and is presented with a problem. We want to know what he's going to do about it. We see him take immediate action. We hear the story of how Oedipus became king and learn something about him. We see him seek the cause of the problem in his land. We see him demand answers when others are warning him that it would be better to forget about it. Most importantly, as he comes closer and closer to the truth, he refuses to back down. He is king and has an obligation. His best quality is what will destroy him, but we see him unflinchingly adhere to his sense that he must find the truth.

All of this is revealed as the plot develops. While you (as author) want to have a pretty precise idea of who your characters are at the outset of your story, it isn't necessary to reveal it all in the first pages. Your reader will stick with you as long as what is happening is interesting.

THE SET-UP

Let's go into a little more detail about what's commonly called the "exposition" or the "set-up." As described earlier, the movement of a plot is from stability to instability and back to stability. A plot can be circular, which means the ending form of stability is nearly identical to the initial situation of stability (Potsie and Richie are friends again). Or, it can be progressive, in which the ending stability is different from the initial situation (Oedipus is no longer king; Creon has replaced him).

Establishing the nature of the initial stability of a story is what the exposition is intended to do. How can a reader understand the struggle that composes the bulk of the story unless they grasp the situation it evolved from?

If we break down an old nursery rhyme, we can see it works like this:

Exposition
There was an old woman who lived in a shoe.
Conflict
She had so many children, she didn't know what to do.
Struggle and resolution
So she gave them some broth without any bread,
Then whipped them all soundly and sent them to bed.

The initial situation is summed up in the first line. In this particular case it is hard to see how living in a shoe relates to the struggle which follows, unless the first line has a meaning like the old woman lives in her shoes (wanders) or that her house is as tight as a shoe. In most illustrations in children's books the shoe is enormous, with windows and a chimney. It doesn't seem much smaller than any peasant cottage, or the little house on the prairie. Still, leaving interpretation to the Mother Goose experts, we recognize the first sentence as an exposition.

If we look at many of the older novels, we find quite elaborate expositions. Almost everyone recalls the famous opening of *A Tale of Two Cities*:

> It was the best of times, it was the worst of times, it was the age of wisdom, it was the age of foolishness, it was the epoch of belief, it was the epoch of incredulity, it was the season of Light, it was the season of Darkness, it was the spring of hope, it was the winter of despair, we had everything before us, we had nothing before us, we were all going direct to Heaven, we were all going direct the other way—in short, the period was

> so far like the present period, that some of its noisiest authorities insisted on its being received, for good or for evil, in the superlative degree of comparison only.
>
> There were a king with a large jaw and a queen with a plain face, on the throne of England; there were a king with a large jaw and a queen with a fair face, on the throne of France. In both countries it was clearer than crystal to the lords of the State preserves of loaves and fishes, that things in general were settled for ever.

Dickens goes on quite a bit after this initial paragraph before he launches into the story of love and politics that will comprise the bulk of his novel. In fact, it isn't until the beginning of his second chapter. He wants you to get the flavor of the times before he starts, as if he were designing the stage set before allowing the actors to enter. Similarly, George Eliot begins her great novel *Silas Marner* with a setting up of the period and circumstances in which her story will play out.

> In the days when the spinning-wheels hummed busily in the farmhouses—and even great ladies, clothed in silk and thread-lace, had their toy spinning-wheels of polished oak—there might be seen in districts far away among the lanes, or deep in the bosom of the hills, certain pallid, undersized men, who, by the side of the brawny country-folk, looked like the remnants of a disinherited race. The shepherd's dog barked fiercely when one of these alien-looking men appeared on the upland, dark against the early winter sunset; for what dog likes a figure bent under a heavy bag?—and these pale men rarely stirred abroad without that mysterious burden. The shepherd himself, though he had good reason to believe that the bag held nothing but flaxen thread, or else the long rolls of strong linen spun from that thread, was not quite sure that this trade of weaving, indispensable though it was, could be carried on entirely without the help of the Evil One. In that far-off time

> superstition clung easily round every person or thing that was at all unwonted, or even intermittent and occasional merely, like the visits of the pedlar or the knife-grinder. No one knew where wandering men had their homes or their origin; and how was a man to be explained unless you at least knew somebody who knew his father and mother?

Eliot's set-up is a bit more to the point as the title character, Silas Marner, will wander into this setting in the paragraph which follows, and, although she is being general, Eliot's description is intended to tell us who Silas Marner is.

I have given you these two long quotations to demonstrate what we mentioned earlier in the book, that elegant diction and superior "music" in your prose may make your reader forgive you on occasion for not getting to the point. These *are* nice passages. However, *A Tale of Two Cities* dates to 1859 and *Silas Marner* to 1861. Readers are not generally as patient as they once were. Being trained by mass media to expect sound bites over content, they also miss many of the finer aspects of good writing. Oh, yes, they may have a lot of patience for Dickens and Eliot and other great writers, but with a new writer? Fuhgeddaboutit! They want to get to the conflict.

Compare the following two opening paragraphs to the previous examples. Both are set in the nineteenth century, but written in the late twentieth by two of the most popular writers of the time. The first is Anne Perry's *A Breach of Promise*.

> Oliver Rathbone leaned back in his chair and let out a sigh of satisfaction. He had just successfully completed a long and tedious case. He had won most substantial damages for his client over a wrongful accusation. The man's name was completely cleared and he was grateful. He had told Rathbone that he was brilliant, and Rathbone had accepted the compliment with grace and appropriate humility, brushing it aside as more a courtesy than truth. But he had worked very hard and

had exercised excellent judgment. He had once again used the skills which had made him one of the finest barristers in London, if not in England.

Notice how quickly we are introduced to this character and how quickly we are thrown into a specific setting and situation, unlike in the earlier examples. Notice how much more cinematic Perry's selection is. Within a few more sentences there will be a knock at the door and the novel will be off at full gallop.

Our second example comes from Elmore Leonard's *Cuba Libre*.

> Tyler arrived with the horses February eighteenth, three days after the battleship *Maine* blew up in Havana harbor. He saw buzzards floating in the sky the way they do but couldn't make out what they were after. This was off Morro Castle, the cattle boat streaming black smoke as it came through the narrows.

Tyler has obviously sailed into trouble and Leonard's careful selection of words creates a vivid picture in the reader's mind while also giving us a feeling for Tyler's speech and thought patterns. In both of these samples, the reader's curiosity is immediately roused and the reader is immersed in a situation, rather than being drawn toward it. Things are already cooking. Something is already happening.

Expositions are generally short these days, if there is much to them at all. They are much more like the set-ups in plays from the past, rather than novels. The mood the author wishes to set, the feeling for the time period which is needed, the rhythms of the language: these things are usually set in the context of an ongoing action. Earlier, we saw how quickly *Oedipus the King* moves into conflict. Shakespeare's theater had little or no scenery and there is usually a brief speech at the beginning of his plays to explain where we are and what the circumstances are. Richard III, for example, explains to the audience in the very first lines of the play what the situation is and what he intends to do, but immediately sets about doing it. A character called

"Chorus" explains the setting of *Henry V*. However, *Macbeth* begins with the witches planning their meeting Macbeth and *The Tempest* with a ship in danger from a storm.

A parody of Shakespeare's *The Taming of the Shrew* was done on the television series *Moonlighting* many years ago and the character of Lucentio kept trying to deliver his lines which provide the exposition for the story of Petruchio and Katherine. In the parody, however, other characters kept interrupting Lucentio until in exasperation he shouted out something like "Give me a break! I'm the exposition!" Surely, this gives us an idea of the impatience of our contemporaries and the problem of directors in dealing with older works. On television, "Padua, 1590" can be titled across the bottom of the screen. A glance at the costumes may tell us the rest of what we need to know for the set-up.

Beginning writers often make the mistake of having too elaborate and involved expositions before beginning the conflict. They try to write like the great writers of the past, rather than like the great writers of the present. We are not writing novels for readers of the mid-nineteenth century. No matter how much we admire and enjoy those novels, their techniques will not work as well with audiences of the twenty-first century. We are better off approximating the kind of plot exposition you get in an old-fashioned drama rather than in an old-fashioned novel.

REVEALING BACKSTORY

So how do we provide the information which might be necessary within our exposition? Consider how movies handle what in Hollywood is called the "backstory." The backstory is everything that has happened to the characters before the movie begins. Say our movie begins with Jack and Jill arguing over who is to take out the garbage. The middle of a fight is often a good place to begin. But who are these people? Where did they come from?

The backstory can be revealed by what they say to each other. Jill says that ever since Jack fell down and broke his crown, he's been too lazy to help her with anything. Jack protests that four years of law school and six years of working in the district attorney's office ought to say who's lazy. Jill responds that she worked two jobs to get him through law school and that if he got a decent salary, they might be able to buy a house and have a child. Remarks like these can reveal much about who these people are and where they've come from.

Also consider how a movie tells you where and when you are. If you see horsemen wearing armor and riding into a castle, you get some sense of the time period. If we see Jack and Jill in an apartment house that looks as shabby as Ralph Kramden's, but has a dishwasher in the kitchenette and a pile of lawbooks on the table, we recognize the time period. Music playing on a radio is a favorite device of writers. Or a news announcement on the television or radio. The headlines of a newspaper. People's clothing. Their manner of speaking. All of these kinds of details can imply a wealth of setting while the characters are engaged in action. The reader will be swept along by the action and not reading a static exposition.

I used the word "imply" above, and implication is often more believable than an outright statement. The right kind of small remark can imply a world. It can serve as a tiny window through which we can see a thousand things. My favorite example of this is in the movie *Dave*. At one point, the president's wife asks Dave whether he was ever married. He says only, "Yes. It didn't work out." Of course, a great deal is implied in the manner in which the actor (Kevin Klein) says this, but the actor's mannerisms are part of the way drama communicates. The brief remark, however, implies a sad struggle in Dave's life that has shaped him. The wording he uses also implies much about his character. He keeps things to himself. He underdramatizes his own hurts. We can't help but feel sorry for him, without feeling that he is weak or deserves pity.

Most beginning writers underestimate the power of implication. They explain too much, especially at the beginning of their novels. If you get the plot moving and feed the readers just enough detail to keep them from feeling lost or confused, they will read on to find out more of the details of the backstory, setting, and premises that constitute the underlying stability that is being undermined by the conflict of the plot.

Notice in the opening words of *My Name is Legion*, how master science fiction writer Roger Zelazny implies so much with so few words:

> I was in the control room when the J-9 unit flaked out on us. I was there for purposes of doing some idiot maintenance work, among other things.
>
> There were two men below in the capsule, inspecting the Highway to Hell, that shaft screwed into the ocean's bottom thousands of fathoms beneath us and soon to be opened for traffic. Ordinarily, I wouldn't have worried, as there were two J-9 technicians on the payroll. Only one of them was on leave in Spitzbergen and the other had entered sick bay just that morning. As a sudden combination of wind and turbulent waters rocked the *Aquina* and I reflected it was now the eve of RUMOKO, I made my decision. I crossed the room and removed a side panel.

A less skilled writer would have explained much of what is implied in this opening and deadened the sensation of forward motion in the plot. What is a J-9? Some kind of technical gizmo. It's important because the narrator reacts to its failure immediately. What it actually does is not as important at this moment as the fact that his reaction proves it is crucial to whatever these men are doing. The first sentence of the second paragraph tells us that we are in some kind of craft on the ocean, and later we find out it is called the *Aquila* that it moves on the water, unlike, say, a rigid oil platform. The references to maintenance work, a payroll, and the technicians on leave implies routine industrial work—not glamorous, but professional. Also note the implications of character in the narrator's choice of words. His professionalism has a tough edge. He can handle himself. He does "idiot" maintenance work. The J-9 "flaked out." The shaft has been nicknamed the "Highway to Hell." We get not only a strong sense of setting

Mastering Plot

and character, but also a feeling for what kind of book this is going to be. Most of the effect, however, is the result of choosing the right words to imply many other things that are not directly said. We are immersed in a plot problem and pick up details as we rush forward.

An example from a very different kind of book is the opening of David Guterson's *Snow Falling on Cedars*.

> The accused man, Kabuo Miyamoto, sat proudly upright with a rigid grace, his palm's placed softly on the defendant's table—the posture of a man who has detached himself insofar as this is possible at his own trial. Some of the gallery would later say that his stillness suggested a disdain for the proceedings; others felt certain it veiled a fear of the verdict that was to come. Whichever it was, Kabuo showed nothing—not even a flicker of the eyes.

The paragraph then shifts into a physical description of Kabuo, but notice how much we have been told by implication. The words "accused" and "defendant's table" tells us we are in a courtroom and a picture of all the rest of that room is created in our minds by just those few words. Later Guterson will describe the courtroom in detail and we may have to revise our imagined setting, but this does not affect us at this moment. If the implications create a seriously different image of the courtroom which has to be drastically revised, the later description could be confusing and irritating for readers. We must be careful what we are implying to avoid this kind of mistake, but, again, explaining too much makes an opening drag.

Other implications in the passage above come from the mention of those in the gallery. People have come. People are speculating about Kabuo's reaction. Therefore, it is a significant trial, not a traffic case or a frivolous law suit. The speculations also imply that the spectators don't really know Kabuo very well and we are getting the sense that he is an alien in the community. As in the Zelazny passage, we have been thrust into the middle of an ongoing situation, with the tensions of a plot up front and moving forward, and with much of it conveyed through implication instead of direct statement.

BRAINSTORMER #5

Go to your bookshelf and select several novels that you have read and enjoyed. Open to the first paragraphs. Ask yourself the following questions about them.

1) Does the author begin in the middle of a scene?
2) Is the primary conflict of the book present and what is it?
3) If so, in what way is it present?
4) Is the mood of the novel suggested in this paragraph?
5) If so, how is it suggested?
6) In what way does the author set the scene?

For example, take the opening two paragraphs of John Le Carré's *The Spy Who Came in from the Cold*:

> The American handed Leamas another cup of coffee and said, "Why don't you go back and sleep? We can ring you if he shows up."
>
> Leamas said nothing, just stared through the window of the checkpoint, along the empty street.

1) Something is happening.
2 & 3) Leamas is a burned out spy. You can feel that in the sleepless ("another cup of coffee"), pointless waiting for someone to cross out of East Berlin.
4 & 5) See 2 & 3. It evokes the emptiness of Cold War espionage.
6) "Checkpoint" immediately suggests Berlin and the Cold War.

This is a brilliant opening, proof that Le Carré deserves his reputation as the master of spy fiction. See if you can find other brilliant openings. Then start writing this way.

Chapter 6
Increasing Intensity

As we move through time further along in the progression of a plot, we expect the tension to build to higher levels of excitement. A reader expects the story to become more intense at each step along the way, until the climax or resolution. At that point, the conflict which has been the overall subject of the novel ends as the primary problem is solved. A story in which the intensity does not rise usually gives the impression that nothing is happening, even though there may be a great many things described in the scenes.

For example, suppose we have a couple Mr. and Mrs. Fisticoff. They argue all the time over ridiculous things, especially on Friday nights when they both drink enough beer to empty the U-Tote-Em's cooler. The Fisticoffs yell. They throw chairs and insults like the riff-raff on afternoon television. They batter each other with household objects, including the electric wok, brooms, ice trays, bags of onions, and the telephone. Frequently, they end up in the emergency room, getting sewn together while a bored police officer asks once again if either wants to press charges. Neither ever does. In fact, heads pounding, they usually lose their anger against each other and begin to berate the police for interfering in their private life.

Each Friday (or holiday) the neighbors can count on shrieking and bellowing and screaming, so most of them just turn up their televisions and shake their heads. There is no question that plenty is going on in the Fisticoff home. There is no question that it is the result of deep-seated conflict which manifests itself with the lubrication of brew. But everyone—especially the long-suffering police who must drive there every weekend—is bored with it. Some of the neighbors can't help themselves and wish one of the Fisticoffs would just kill the other, so that this monotony would end. The "story" which could be made of the Fisticoffs' lives is full of action, but goes nowhere. The stakes get no higher from week to week. The use of different objects as weapons doesn't change the basic outcome.

Imagine the Fisticoff story as four hundred pages of twenty page chapters in which each chapter contains a fight. The novel begins with Vern Fisticoff going to the U-Tote-Em for beer, and ends with Irma Fisticoff going to the U-Tote-Em for beer. How many fights would you read before you put the novel down? If the writer were a brilliant comic writer, or an amazingly adept realist, she might keep you engaged for longer than a less skillful writer. However, even if you hung in, and read all the way to the end, wouldn't you still feel cheated?

Is that it? you'd be asking with exasperation. What's the point? The point is pointlessness? Not much to that concept, is there? Short of cooking up some existential explanation in an attempt to justify this flatlined story, you'd feel like you wasted your time. And even in the most famous absurdist and existential dramas in which nothing much happens in the usual sense (such as *Waiting for Godot*, *Steambath*, or *No Exit*) there is usually an increase in the mental tension as the characters gradually attempt to address their problem. That is at least partly why these dramas are much more interesting than those by imitators who only understand the philosophical concept and not the need of rising intensity.

SCENES AND CHAPTERS

A novel develops through a series of units, usually chapters, which are composed of one or more scenes. As you've no doubt seen, some writers use chapters as units and give each a separate title. Some writers prefer to put a space, asterisk, number, or some other divider between units. Occasionally, there are novels that had no divisions at all, such as Gabriel García Márquez's *The Autumn of the Patriarch*, which doesn't even have paragraph breaks. That kind of wall-to-wall prose is more than a little daunting. Many people I know who adore García Márquez's writing couldn't force themselves to finish that one. We all like a convenient stopping place when the night has gotten long and we'd like to put the book aside. But despite all the care with which writers may title their units and designers may separate them, none of these things matter much as far as plotting is concerned.

What is important is that however you divide up your novel or separate its units, these units should have a solid structural basis which reflects the overall novel's structure. Each scene and chapter should be organized to behave as a mini-story. It should begin with a hook to catch the reader's interest, have a specific struggle or problem which is being worked out, move through a rising intensity, and then reach a conclusion which can serve as the impetus for the scene or chapter which follows. The more memorable it is in itself, the more it will contribute to our general sense that the whole novel is compelling. To go back to our metaphor of building a house, each wall must have its own sturdy structure so that all of the walls together can make a sturdy house.

Most of the suggestions about how to create a good plot also apply to how to create a good chapter. Beginning *in medias res*, giving an immediate sense that there is conflict, and keeping a sense of forward motion, are some of these. A chapter usually cannot stand on its own, however, or the story becomes too episodic or unfocussed. Each unit should be an element of our larger plot, connecting two parts of it. The beginning of a chapter should seem to have arisen naturally from what came before, even though there may be a gap of centuries between chapters. The end of a chapter (or unit) should throw the reader towards the next unit of the plot, the following scene and chapter.

CLIFFHANGING

For centuries, a favorite technique of writers has been to end a chapter by breaking the last scene before it reaches a climax, then presenting the climax later. This has come to be called "cliffhanging," from the melodramatic film serials of the 1920s and later. Weekly episodes of *The Perils of Pauline*, *Flash Gordon*, *Captain Marvel*, and many others became a regular part of the movie experience up until the 1950s. Presented in twenty-minute "chapters" over twenty weeks, these stories of adventure concluded each episode with a major character in obvious danger, such as hanging from the edge of a cliff. When the next episode began, the character would be saved, the plot would advance some more, and then the same, or other, character or characters would find themselves in immediate mortal peril.

As Episode 10 ended, you might see the detective hero struggling with one of the evil henchmen for control of an automobile. The car swerves, goes off the road, flies out over a canyon, and smashes in flames to the rocks below. A week later, Episode 11 would begin with the same struggle going on in the car. It swerves, but as it goes off the road, the hero rolls out of his door onto the pavement. The car flies into the canyon and smashes in flames as before.

Sure, it's a cheap trick splitting off in the middle of the action, but it brought people back to see how the hero could escape from such a terrible situation. Sometimes if you see these episodes back to back, you can see that the ending of the first is different from the beginning of the second, but with a week's gap between episodes, the producers assumed the audience's memory would blur somewhat.

You can also use the cliffhanging technique to help the forward motion of your novels. Simply think of it as ending *in medias res*, rather than beginning *in medias res*. In your plot outline, you will likely have a number of incidents which compose neat little units. You can break these off at a high moment in the unit.

AN EXAMPLE

Chapter One of *Penny Pinching* by Susan Moody begins (*in medias res*) with the discovery of a body. Barnaby Midas has just risen from the bed beside his lover Penny Wanawake to enjoy the ocean view outside the window. A young and beautiful woman, almost identical to Penny in appearance, has been brained out there. It doesn't take them long to figure out that someone probably killed her thinking that she was Penny. The chapter ends as follows, the two undressed and upset lovers still trying to deal with their gruesome discovery:

> "I don't get a kick out of dead bodies, you know," he said.
> "Hey," Penny said softly. "Hey."
> He turned. She walked towards him. "Neither do I," she said. "But I get a kick out of you."
> Across her breasts shimmered the four big letters. He took his time reading them. L. O. V. E., they said. They moved into each other's arms. Held each other. Tightly.
> Inside the house, the telephone began to cry.

It sounds like an ending: the discovery of the body is over, and the lovers clutch each other. The telephone ringing in the final sentence hangs small questions in the air, however. Who is calling? Why?

We turn to the next page to find out. The story question of who killed the woman outside the window is already hanging in the air. That is a question for the entire novel to answer. However, the smaller question raised by the telephone beginning "to cry" (an especially expressive word at this point) provokes the turning of the page. It's a cliffhanger. Oh, a subtler cliffhanger than driving a Packard off a precipice, but still a cliffhanger.

As chapter two begins, we discover we are not finished with the scene which began in chapter one:

> By the time Penny reached it, it had stopped ringing.
> "Perhaps it was the cops," Barnaby said, "saying they can't make it after all." He could feel his insides beginning to clench. He wished he hadn't seen so many movies where someone is thrown into jail and has a hell of a job proving his innocence. Particularly since he couldn't remember when he'd last been innocent.

The next paragraph switches to Penny's point of view as she mulls the possibility that her lover might have been involved with the murder. She decides she loves him and trusts him, considering that the murderer might have intended some kind of payback or revenge against Barnaby. The scene ends as Penny feels grateful to whatever God is out there that she was not the victim. There is a break (but not a chapter break), and then the next scene begins (again *in medias res*) with a detective questioning Barnaby.

It is easy to see how the use of simple techniques helps to increase the forward motion of the novel. The natural inclination of a writer might be to do the first scene as chapter one, then begin chapter two with the detective. But by breaking off the scene at an important moment, the reader may be drawn into chapter two. The rest of the scene which began the book ends quickly in chapter two, but by then readers will not be as inclined to put down the book. They will go on to the end of chapter two—which, by the way, does not have a cliffhanger. It ends during a conversation without showing us the details of characters exiting, but those details have nothing to do with the story. Knowing what *not* to say is one of a good writer's best attributes. Who cares that they left the room? Of course they did. As chapter three begins Penny is in San Francisco.

And what of the telephone ringing? The readers of a Penny Wanawake mystery are already very alert to every detail, hoping to figure out "who done it" before Penny does. The position of the ringing in the cliffhanger and at the beginning of chapter two will be memorable. A lot of attention is drawn to it by Barnaby's remark. Readers would immediately suspect that the telephone ringing is not a mere accident which jangles the lovers' nerves. And it shouldn't be, in the ideal plot. Something as prominent as it is, should come back later as a clue or another factor in the chain of events.

Thus, though cliffhanging is a tried and true technique to keep your pot boiling, the event which breaks off the scene should not be accidental or merely attention getting. It should follow the same rules as an attention-getting opening and not mislead. You don't begin a

Mastering Plot

book about a loving family growing up in a small town with a scene more appropriate to the opening of a horror novel. Of course, having a throat ripped out is attention-getting, but it can be inconsistent with the tone and atmosphere of many types of novels. The telephone ringing in our example is attention-getting, but is also appropriate to the context and should integrate into the plot.

CLIFFHANGING VARIATIONS

Allow me to give one more example of cliffhanging. This type doesn't revolve around an action, but a statement. The statement promises conflict which has not yet appeared and usually appears in the form of an observation from the author or a remark by a character. Observations by the author are usually considered either very old fashioned or very postmodern. Commercial authors who are realists usually avoid them, preferring to comment by implication or through the mouths of characters. Instead of writing, "John was a weak man," they show him being weak or have a narrator or another character say it. Hanging a statement on the cliff between chapters is usually a promise by the author that things are going to liven up.

Anthony Trollope's first chapter of *Dr. Wortle's School* is primarily a description of how Rev. Jeffrey Wortle came to become a headmaster and some details of the school he administers. It is rather typical way in which many Victorian novels begin, with a detailed description of setting and character. At the end of the chapter, the grounds are being described, leading the reader to an apartment attached to school building. Trollope concludes as follows:

> It had been the Doctor's scheme to find a married gentleman to occupy this house, whose wife should receive a separate salary for looking after the linen and acting as matron to the school,—doing what his wife did till he became successful,—while the husband should be in orders and take part of the church duties as a second curate. But there had been a difficulty in this.

The long sentence sets you up for the punch of the short sentence, which promises more lively doings in subsequent chapters. Trollope immediately in the next chapter begins to explain some of Dr. Wortle's difficulties. These will become quite severe when it is discovered that the gentleman he hires is not legally married to his wife. Dr. Wortle's kindliness nearly causes him to lose his school and everything he has worked for. His little problem at the beginning builds into one which nearly destroys him.

The author's commenting on the action is appropriate in some kinds of novels and not in others. However, most readers would agree that when the end of a chapter uses the old device of "little did he know," the writer is getting pretty hokey. Usually this is used when the writer realizes that the chapter is grinding to an uninteresting close and wants to raise the voltage by promising later rewards. There isn't anything wrong with that impulse, but "little did he know" is a cheap patch to a bigger problem: a chapter with insufficient life in it.

Usually it goes something like Trollope's opening chapter described above. A character, let's say, Irma Flutewaffle moves to a new town after her divorce. She rents Schnorrer Cottage in rural Dorset and redecorates it in a manner that suits her dream of how she wants to live now, totally independent. She never wants to put up with an inconsiderate man again. She wants to eat when she feels like it, putter in her garden, and baby her schnauzer, Stinky. We read about her perennials and her annuals and her calico sofa. We read about her fixing her drippy faucet and how content she is sitting in her back yard with a cup of Earl Grey and a crumpet. Life is good, Irma is content, and Stinky snores on the hearth.

So do we. Everything is descriptive. There is no problem to engage us, no conflict to stir the blood. The author, sensing this, tries to save the sinking boat. He wants to let us know that excitement is in the offing, so we find an ending to the chapter like this:

> Irma had rediscovered the joys of the solitary life and imagined herself aging quietly in cozy Schnorrer Cottage. Little did

Irma know, however, that by Boxing Day, she would be hopelessly in love with the Soviet Union's most dangerous spy.

Often, this takes the tack that by morning or next Thursday our happy character (little does he or she know!) will be dead. The irony of "little did he know" is obvious and supposedly profound. It tries to catch the same tragic sense of the end of *Oedipus the King*, which warns that we should "Count no man happy until he is dead." But rather than coming out as tragic inevitability, the irony of this forced ending seems comic. It's a terrible joke on the protagonist. She's fancied up in her evening dress and is about to get in a pie fight.

This is another example where inconsistency hurts. If the preceding chapter stays close to Irma's point of view, the sudden appearance of the author at Schnorrer Cottage seems as if the author didn't plan very well. It would be better to begin the chapter by opening with the trump card.

> The Wednesday before the body of Irma Flutewaffle was found dead among her chrysanthemums, she had purchased calico to redecorate her antique settee. Elmore, her ex-husband, had in their twenty-five years of marriage spilled far too much claret on the original brocade for it ever to be clean again. Stinky, her schnauzer, had done his share of damage to the cloth as well, but at least Stinky didn't do it in carelessness. No, calico was the solution. A bright pattern that matched the airy brightness of Schnorrer Cottage.

Obviously, it will be a while before we get back to the murder mentioned in the first sentence, but it will make the mundane details a little more lively until we do. The Victorian novelist Charles Reade once advised writers, "Make them laugh! Make them cry! Make them wait!" Doing it this way at least implies that the author didn't think of it at the last moment. To my taste it would be far better to fill in the details of life at Schnorrer Cottage while Irma's murder is being investigated. In other words, start later in the plot line.

"Little did he know" should generally be avoided. It isn't foreshadowing as much as it is "forced shadowing." It's the punch line of a cheap joke that tells the reader, "Ha! All those pages didn't mean a thing. Aren't I clever?" Readers never appreciate deception.

THE TAG LINE

Similarly, a character speaking at the end of a chapter might promise interesting things in the pages to follow. An example of this is in the novel *A Modern Romance* by Winston Churchill. No, this is not Churchill the statesman, trivia fans, but one of the most successful American novelists at the beginning of the twentieth century. He was the Stephen King of his day and had many best sellers. At the end of one of the later chapters, a character named Hugh is sailing with the woman he loves to his estate.

> "I can't wait to show it to you, Honora,—to see you in it," he exclaimed. "I have so long pictured you there and our life as it will be."

Maybe it's better for Churchill to remain in eclipse, but, however bad his wording might be, his technique is sound. While not as ominous as Trollope's wording or a startling as the phone ringing, there is still a distinct sense that things are going to happen when Honora gets there, and inquiring minds want to know what they will be. The last sentence creates anticipation for what is to come.

Numerous authors also end their chapters (or story units) in mid-dialog. A conversation is going on as part of the plot. All of the significant information which is to be conveyed in the scene has been presented. A character says a line which is interesting and promises future action, then the chapter abruptly ends. In the theater and motion pictures, this kind of line ending a speech or a scene is called the "tag

Mastering Plot

line," and it often intended as a cue to another actor. Think of your tag lines in this way, as cues to further action in your plot.

Here is the end of a section in great Canadian author Robertson Davies' *The Lyre of Orpheus*. They are discussing a composer in residence who is coming to supervise the finishing of an incomplete opera by nineteenth-century composer E. T. A. Hoffman:

> "From what point of the compass does this avatar appear?" asked Arthur.
> "From Stockholm. Doesn't the name tip you off?" [said Penny]
> "We are greatly privileged to have her, I suppose?"
> "Can't say. Is she a Snark or a Boojum? Only time will tell."

Davies doesn't give us the rest of the conversation or describe people getting their coats to go home. He leaves us with this curious tag line referring to imaginary creatures created by Lewis Carroll in *The Hunting of the Snark*. The line is something that Penny would say and the other characters present would appreciate as well-educated, upper-class Canadians, so it seems natural to the character. Later, there is a detailed discussion of the snark and boojum to satisfy the curiosity of readers who want to know why the woman is referred to in this way. But, on the fundamental level of moving the plot, it also presents the reader with curiosity about the woman who is coming—she doesn't actually show up for many pages. Is she a snark or a boojum?

Examples of this kind of tag line are common, but let's look at one more. In Clyde Edgerton's *Killer Diller*, a young man named Wesley is with a girl he adores, Phoebe. Her father doesn't approve of their relationship: Wesley is a "wayward youth," while Phoebe is enrolled in a Christian weight-loss clinic nearby. As this chapter ends, they are in a car and Wesley has nervously kissed her for the first time. He accidentally chokes on the toothpick he has been holding in his mouth and coughs in a frightening manner, but assures Phoebe he is okay, that the toothpick is on the floorboard. Phoebe thinks a used toothpick on the floor is nasty.

"I'll get it." Wesley reaches down to the floorboard, pretends to pick up a toothpick. He rolls down the window and pretends to throw it outside. He rolls the window back up and looks at Phoebe. "Now. Where were we at?"

The comedy of the scene is gentle and affectionate. We like these kids, though Wesley's pretense of disposing of the toothpick reveals the con-man aspect of his character. The plot has advanced because, as her father fears, Phoebe has fallen for Wesley, which is going to create problems. The tag line, like many tag lines in romantic situations that are heating up, implies what is to follow. But there is no point in describing these two making out in their awkward way. The fact that they are in love is the plot problem. Although the situations are very different in Davies' and Edgerton's novels, the use of the technique serves the same purposes: raising curiosity about what will happen. Both authors know that the essential information of the scene has been sent and so they quickly end.

Also, one of the qualities of good writing is implying the existence of things outside and beyond the venue of the scene. If a scene in an office building in New York City is done right, we will always feel the presence of that great city. Breaking dialog (or any scene, for that matter) at the right point, can convey all the reader needs to know to advance the story, and create curiosity about what is to come, but it can also leave the impression that there is more in the world created by the novel than is on the page.

We know that the characters talked on. That they finished their drinks and took a cab home. That they talked sweetly for hours, kissing and feeling the first flush of love. The incompleteness of the dialog or scene is completed in our imaginations, not in specific detail, but in a feeling. We have the sense of what we don't see and we feel its presence. The dialog that appears to be incomplete feels complete. It works like that which Ernest Hemingway spoke of when he said that a story should be like an iceberg, mostly submerged. The part that sticks up makes up feel the power of what we cannot see, under the water.

LEITMOTIFS

Another technique for building intensity during the long journey of a novel is to use repeating images, phrases, themes, and thoughts. As each repeats it registers more strongly with the reader creating both a cumulative effect, as well as contributing to the impression of the plot as a whole unit. The term for these repetitions I like to use is borrowed from music.

Richard Wagner's operas are legendary for their length, but they are among the greatest dramatic musical spectacles ever created. *The Ring of the Nibelungen* consists of four operas which tell the story of the theft of gold from the Rhine and how this crime brings about the destruction of the gods. The complete *Ring* takes fourteen to seventeen hours, but—you guessed it—it is a single plot. Each of the four operas emphasizes different characters and each has the ability to be performed alone, but they are all linked. The *Ring* has musical unity and a unity of plot.

One of the ways in which Wagner achieved unity in this enormous cycle is the use of what he called the leitmotif (or *leitmotiv*). Translated, the word means a "leading or dominant theme," but the word has come to be used in its original form in English. What he did in the music was to associate certain musical passages with certain characters, objects, events, and emotions in the drama. These passages would appear at appropriate moments throughout the *Ring*, and become more elaborate or meaningful at each appearance.

For example, there is a leitmotif associated with the hero Siegfried. It, of course, is used when he appears in the drama, but also appears before he is born, when a character might allude to something that will require Siegfried in the future of the story. These touches pass into the audience's ears and are planted in their minds. When the full theme manifests itself, or when Siegfried appears in his full power, there is a sense it was inevitable. It seems familiar, though perhaps only in a subconscious way, and helps provide a feeling of unity.

Although novelists can't use musical notes directly, they can use the technique of the leitmotif to create a sense of unity in their plots.

Leitmotifs which appear early in the novel and recur throughout will make the plot seem very well-constructed. Remember that we earlier discussed how the conclusion of a story must seem to have developed naturally from the beginning. The audience likes to feel that the author contrived and created the story as a whole. It should be logical and inevitable, but not predictable.

How can you use leitmotifs in your novel? One example which critics have discussed is the way that Ernest Hemingway uses rain as a motif for sadness in *A Farewell to Arms*. Each time it is raining in that novel, sad events are unfolding. At the conclusion of the novel, as it should, it has its moment of greatest emotional intensity. The woman for whom the hero has given up so much dies. Little is said about his feelings at that moment, though we know he is devastated.

> After a while I went out and left the hospital and walked back
> to the hotel in the rain.

That's all it says. The fact that he walks away in the rain is incredibly sad because of the repetition of the motif in the earlier parts of the novel.

Hemingway doesn't beat us over the head with "the rain is sad," "the rain is sad." It may seem a detail in the earlier uses, just part of the surroundings. It fits naturally with whatever is going on at that moment. But it accumulates by repetition, dripping like rain–*pat! pat!*–producing a powerful emotional effect.

The pacing of leitmotifs is important. If they recur too often, the reader may get annoyed and think, "Yeah, yeah, yadda, yadda. Enough already." If they occur at too widely spaced intervals, the reader may have forgotten the detail, and the repetition will have no effect except on people with unusually lengthy memories.

Often the leitmotif is a useful way to build character over the course of a story. For example, we have a character of some ordinary occupation. Let's say Jack Drudge is an accountant for the state tax services. Early in the book, he is at a party and something in the conversation provokes him to say, "I was a quarterback in high school. Third string, but I got to play."

The first time he says it, it will not have much meaning. It seems to be just an offhand remark. But suppose he says it again, in a different context, maybe at his office to his boss. The second time it comes up, perhaps in a context that doesn't immediately invite an association with football, the reader will be clued in that it has significance of some kind. You see, readers don't expect their storytellers to be sloppy types who repeat details for no reason. What does the remark really mean? They turn on their radar. They wait.

Look, here comes the remark again, this time when he is talking to his son about math homework. The son says, "Yeah, I know." He's heard it a few too many times. Now the reader is certain it is a significant clue to Jack Drudge's character. When does he mention it? Suppose it seems to be connected to the dullness of his current life. Aha! Jack thinks back on his high school football days as the only time in his life when he did anything glorious or meaningful. His moments on the third string were the only moments of his life that make him feel good about his life. By alluding to this at different moments of the plot, the writer creates a thread of meaning that weaves through the story, connecting disparate elements, and creating a feeling of plot unity and character consistency.

It often isn't necessary that there be more explanation of the remark. In fact, it is usually more evocative if the remark is a bit mysterious. That way the reader gets curious about it and tries to interpret it. If it is too mysterious, this won't work, of course, because the fact will be obscure, not just mysterious. It will frustrate the reader trying to assimilate the meaning of it. At the other extreme, motion pictures are often particularly tiresome in over-explaining everything. The character that explains that he is an alcoholic because he grew up in a family of alcoholics is a bit too aware of his own psychology to be believable. If he understood himself that well, he shouldn't have a problem, should he?

On the other hand, if we use Jack Drudge's brief football career as a leitmotif, it would be perfectly acceptable and perhaps add new dimension to his character if the leitmotif changes slightly as it reappears. That's what Wagner did in musical terms. Musical phrases at the beginning of the *Ring*, recur and evolve through all fifteen hours. The "Nature motif" becomes the "Rhine motif" and so on. Suppose the first appearance of the motif tells us that Jack was a third string quarterback. A later appearance adds that he played, but only in two games. The shift lets us know that we haven't quite understood the full meaning of the leitmotif.

A later appearance of the leitmotif tells us that he was sent in to take the snap, kneel down, waste the last few seconds of the game, and preserve a slim lead. But, like the notorious Joe Pisarcik of the New York Giants, Jack fumbled and the other team ran it ninety yards for the score and victory. Now we know that Jack's memory is not of glory, but of humiliation. He has a sense (perhaps) that he is incapable of doing anything right. He is a schlump in his own mind and will always be a schlump. The best writers wouldn't over-explain or analyze this, but simply allow the facts to imply the meaning.

Leitmotifs need not be thematic or biographical. They can simply be part of the setting. Repeated references to an old oak at the front of a farmhouse, for example, might reinforce the idea of the solidity of the family that grows up beneath its branches. Or it might stand in ironic contrast to the fragmenting, dysfunctional family that lives inside the house. The landscape of the moors surrounding the house in *The Hound of the Baskervilles* implies the dark and treacherous secrets that lead to the murders that Sherlock Holmes must investigate.

Using the leitmotif is not purely a matter of plotting. There are obviously overtones of symbolism, characterization, and setting. They should never seem tacked on to the characters as an artificial way of making them interesting. They should arise naturally from the circumstances and surroundings of the novel, without being clichés. We've had quite enough of the Irishman who is always looking for a drink and the fundamentalist who is weirdly sexually warped. A plot that speeds down an overused highway is unlikely to provide an interesting trip. Head off looking for back roads and dimly lit alleys.

The spacing of leitmotif appearances and the number of different leitmotifs employed is largely a matter of instinct. As always, it is difficult for the writer to gauge precisely how many are too many or how often is too often. If there are too many different leitmotifs used, they will lose impact. The reader won't likely be able to keep them all in mind and each one will be diminished in a kind of supply and demand. A lot of different threads will seem individually less important, than a few powerful threads.

The magnitude of the leitmotifs is also a factor. Trying to get big meaning into a vessel that will not hold it is a mistake. Nothing is more amateurish than the way beginning writers often try to find the meaning of life in some minor experience. In the Renaissance, it was believed that there were astronomical signs when great men were born or died, but we find it a little hard to accept that the universe changed because your girlfriend ditched you or your dishwasher blew up. Some writers might be able to get more out of minor events than others, but remember that overdramatizing can become pretty funny.

THE PAUSE THAT REFRESHES

Increasing intensity is crucial to an effective plot, but it is possible to reach a point of diminishing returns. Imagine a symphony which begins at high volume. In a Beethoven-like or Wagnerian fashion, it thunders out from the first chord and continues on in that way for ninety minutes. Imagine a movie about an aircraft carrier which begins with a stupendous dogfight which lasts through the entire movie. Or imagine an actor playing Hamlet or Stanley Kowalski or any other character, who shouts from curtain to curtain. All of these things would be awful as either art or entertainment.

Edgar Allan Poe described the short story as a piece of fiction which can be read at one sitting and produces a single effect—with him, of course, terror. When done well, as in Poe's "The Black Cat" or "The Tell-Tale Heart," the single effect lingers in the mind for years. But it would take an ironclad rump to read a novel in one sitting. And if we got only one effect from our five or more hours of marathon reading, the single effect might be a sense of wasted time. Even the greatest excitement and most spectacular events can become wearying if they are relentless. I remember hearing one disgruntled movie-goer whisper to his wife sometime around the third hour of *Titanic*, "When is this dang boat gonna sink, fer pity's sake?" Plainly the special effects had lost their specialness for him.

Any lengthy or large work of art needs shifts in tone and intensity to maintain interest. Sure, Beethoven's "Ode to Joy" at the end of his Symphony No. 9 is an explosion of sound. It is a tsunami when the full orchestra and chorus cuts loose. But there are quiet moments building to this climax, moments when single instruments give moments of simple beauty. Wagner is probably most famous for the "Ride of the Valkyries" in *Die Walküre*, a selection that was used memorably in the attack scene in the movie *Apocalypse Now*. But Wagnerian operas are not a relentless succession of Valkyrie rides.

Think of any concert, and notice how the band or singer varies the types of songs, going from fast to slow, from sad to funny. The first task of a screenwriter adapting a play is to think about how the scenes can be moved from place to place to create visual interest. Playwrights, who cannot vary setting that easily, exploit lighting and costume and changes in the dialog. Painters insert comic sights into some very serious canvases, and vice versa. Even the landscape designer puts variations in plants at certain points so that visual monotony can be avoided.

So also with novels. Too much of the same is monotonous, so novelists use a variety of characters. They usually try to vary settings. They change the speed of the language, such as using quick, short

Mastering Plot

sentences for action passages, and long sentences for descriptive ones. They have different characters speak in a slightly different manner. They may use different points of view and different levels of diction, having one section larded with sixty-four dollar words while the next is in the jargon of a military officer.

Too much of the same in plot is monotonous also. The writer who has one unremittingly, relentlessly exciting scene following another can wear out the reader. Too much shouting makes us deaf, and shouting even louder after that will not be heard because of the deafness. A change of pace is often what is needed to make the rising intensity of the plot effective. The reader might like to catch her breath before taking the final climb.

An excellent example of varying the mood occurs in William Shakespeare's *Macbeth*. As you may recall, the play begins with a battle going on in which Macbeth triumphs over the enemies of King Duncan. After the battle, however, Macbeth encounters three witches who predict he will become king. Once this idea becomes planted in his head, Macbeth feels pressure to make it true. Lady Macbeth in particular urges him to make the prophecy come true and whatever queasiness the warrior feels about using murder to achieve the crown is gradually overcome. In a scene of great madness and passion, Macbeth finally brings himself to murder Duncan and Lady Macbeth smears Duncan's blood on the king's grooms to frame them.

The emotional power of this scene is so strong the play is in danger of burning up, like a wire with too many volts passing through it. But, we've just started. We are going to move on to higher levels of madness and passion. Macbeth will feel forced to murder his best friend and the children of his enemy Macduff, he will see a bloody ghost at his dinner table, and Lady Macbeth will deteriorate into insanity. By play's end, Macbeth's severed head will be on the end of a pike. It can easily turn into too much.

Yet, in the manipulation of this frenzied, hyperbolic plot, we get another glimpse of the great storyteller's genius. Shakespeare builds up powerful intensity through these events leading up to until Duncan's murder. Someone begins knocking at the door and Lady Macbeth says they must go back to bed and pretend to be sleeping. Macbeth, who suddenly sees the monstrosity of his own act, says, "To know my deed, 'twere best not to know myself. Wake Duncan with thy knocking! I would thou couldst!" He exits. At that point Shakespeare seems to recognize that he may have the audience so tightly wound that they cannot bear any greater feelings. So what does he do? He inserts a scene to bring them back down to where they began.

The knocking continues, but it arouses a porter. The porter engages in a hung-over monologue about the gate being the entrance of Hell and speculates as to the type of sinner that is trying so hard to get in. When he finally opens the gate, Macduff and the Earl of Lennox enter and the porter explains that there was too much carousing the night before. Drink, he says is a great provoker of three things: nose painting, sleep and urine. "Lechery, sir," he continues famously, "it provokes and unprovokes. It provokes the desire, but it takes away the performance." Funny stuff! Macduff and Lennox are in a light-hearted mood. It is not until Macduff sees the bodies inside that all of this frippery ends.

Yes, the audience knows through the entire scene what the lords are about to find, but the low humor of the porter changes the mood drastically. Now that the audience is relaxed again, Shakespeare can begin raising the voltage up to the high levels of the ending. A scene which on first reading might be thought to be unimportant, or just plain silly, becomes an important part of the structural scheme of the play. The roller coaster drops you down before bringing you up for the final climb.

ANOTHER MOOD SHIFT

Let's take an example from a novel. Almost any novel will exhibit deliberate shifts from intensity to quietness along the overall rise to climax. *Lady With a Laptop* by D. M. Thomas is a humorous book about a writing teacher who is part of a summer workshop on a Greek island. There are a variety of odd characters taking the workshop and one of them, Lucinda, is found dead in her room. Because she might be a suicide, the locals refuse to dig a grave or do a burial at sea from a boat. The only choice is to drop the coffin from a cliff into the sea. In the scene ending Part I of the novel, they take the coffin at dawn to the precipice. A small ceremony is enacted, then Lucinda's coffin is shoved over the edge. Unfortunately, as it plummets toward the sea, it strikes a projecting rock and bursts open. Thomas describes it brilliantly.

> We see, with horror, Lucinda appear, tumbling, her familiar brown divided skirt keeping her decent, a white polo-necked sweater we hadn't seen, and falling—limbs flailing like a rag doll's, along with stones, the broken pieces of a coffin, a radio, a laptop computer (her sister has requested that those precious objects be with her)—falling, falling, and at last vanishing beneath the swirling foam.

The funeral party screams and weeps at the sight, then Thomas ends the chapter with a brief and slightly comic apology by the man who arranged the funeral. This is the technique we discussed earlier, in which we break in the middle of dialog.

However, even with the punch line of the apology, the scene is certainly highly emotional and very intense, while being gruesomely funny as well. Part I thus ends on a high note, a mini-climax. When we turn to Part II, which immediately follows, the mood shifts, though the comic feeling is maintained. Thomas comes back to one of the absurd meetings which the workshop holds each morning. An excitable young man with jug ears speaks of the healing powers of the island, praises one of his teachers, and those who prepared the vegetarian food. He thanks just about everyone, and "receives a big clap.". It is all superficial, silly, and stupidly sincere. Thus the routine of the workshop is re-established, the excitement subsides, and the reader can anticipate another upward swing.

After you put your story outline together, always consider the intensity of feeling in adjacent scenes. You've got another writer's balancing act to perform: 1) the general trend of your line of scenes (units) should be upward, but 2) there should be units which lower the intensity momentarily, allowing readers to catch their breath. You should have more "up's" than "down's." You shouldn't be going:

UP / DOWN / UP / DOWN / UP / DOWN / UP

But more like:

UP / UP / UP / DOWN / UP / UP / DOWN / UP / UP/ UP

The example has three "up's" to a "down," but there's no definite pattern you need to follow. It depends on the length of the scenes and how far up in intensity a particular scene might go. Don't write a "down" scene just because you want to maintain a pattern, but only when you feel a change of pace is called for. Trust your instincts. Readers don't care about your patterns, they care about story. The story always comes first.

BRAINSTORMER #6

Take your story outline and give each scene in it a voltage on a scale from one (1) to ten (10), in which one is the least intense in emotion and ten is the most intense. Consider each scene or chapter independently, grading it as a whole. A scene which is entirely descriptive, setting scene, or depicting a character in unproductive thought, might receive a one. A ten might be the Battle of the Marne or a scene in which the lovers finally, passionately fall into each other's arms (think Rhett carrying Scarlett up the staircase in *Gone With the Wind*).

119

Get some graph paper and make an intensity graph of your story outline. You will probably have more scenes than the sample below, but if it comes out in a general way similar to the sample, you probably have a pretty good story, as far as intensity manipulation goes.

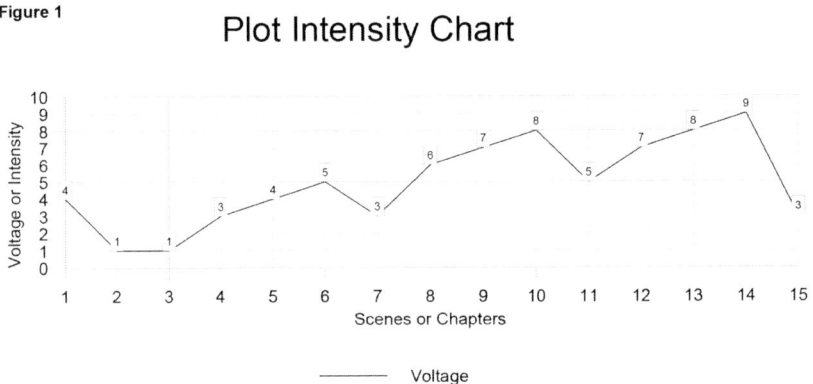

Figure 1

In Figure 1, we see that this writer has no scenes of zero voltage. Every scene should have *some* conflict or intensity. No matter how much you might love your writing in a scene in which nothing happens, either make something happen or throw it out. No zeroes! Ever!

Scene 1 begins with 4 level intensity to engage the readers' interest. This should be strong enough to carry the interest through Scenes 2 and 3. Scenes 4, 5, and 6 build up to a mini-climax, then 7 drops back a bit. 8, 9, 10, and 11 follow a similar pattern, but are higher than earlier scenes. 12 and 13 build up to the big climax scene in 14. 15 is a brief anticlimax or dénouement—loose ends are tied up, the main characters live happily ever after, that sort of thing.

We can see here that the later scenes are on average more intense than the early scenes and the general trend is up, with a few dips for interest's sake.

If your graph looks something like the Figure 2, you're in for a bit of work.

Figure 2

The beginning is so slow, you'll be lucky to have a reader to the third scene. If anyone manages to drag themselves to scene 10, the sudden intensity of it will likely not be absorbed. That voltage surge will burn up the wires and your readers will be stunned. What was *that*? It will seem bizarre. Following this jolt, the novel drags through five not-intense scenes, a very dull ending. If your reader finishes this novel, she will do it strictly out of duty, won't enjoy it, and will forget it quickly.

What is needed? To begin with, moving that intense scene 10 further back towards the ending. Eliminating some scenes after scene 10 or compressing them into one another. Other scenes will need to be intensified, perhaps by adding additional elements, or by altering characters so that the price they are paying for being true to themselves is far more serious.

Mastering Plot

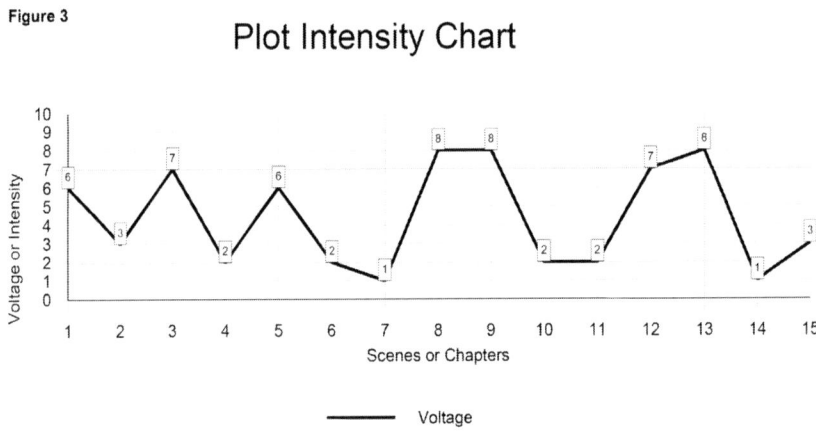

Figure 3

Does your graph look something like Figure 3? What a roller coaster ride! The reader will hardly know what to make of this kind of high voltage/brownout alternation. Strangely, this can be as monotonous as a nearly flat graph. That high intensity first scene might be an excellent way to start, and the drop down in the second scene would work well, but the ups and downs don't produce an overall upward trend. By the time the third or fourth high intensity scene appears, the reader will be reacting to it with a yawn. Oh, this again.

Try this exercise with your own story outline, or, if you feel you're not capable of being impartial enough, try it out on a novel you admire. If you don't see in a successfully published novel the general upward trend and variation in intensity that has been described in this chapter that novel is very unusual. Try it on a novel that leaves you cold. Although its problems might derive from other things than the story structure, you may see that the final chapters, say, fall in intensity, or that it does not build in a successful way.

Once you've done this exercise a couple of times, you will automatically do it in your head when you're composing your novel, and you usually won't need to do it so meticulously.

BRAINSTORMER #7

Take a novel you really love. See if you find any repeating images, expressions, actions, or any other kind of leitmotif. Mark their appearances, using colored pencils or Post-It notes.

Consider how far apart they are spaced in the novel. Notice how naturally (or unnaturally) they arise from the context and reflect it. Notice how casually they are introduced and employed, how you might not notice them if you weren't looking for them.

Do this with several books you admire, particularly with those types of novels you'd like to write.

Chapter 7
The Ending

Failing to end your novel when the struggle is over is a common mistake beginning novelists often make. As the beginning of a plot is the point at which the struggle commences, the end, of course, is the point at which the chain of causal events reaches a resolution. When the anger of Achilles is finally assuaged and he takes pity on the old king Priam begging for his son's body, the plotline has ended. When the murderer confesses his crime or the lovers fall into each other's arms or the hero dies of his wounds, the struggle has resolved.

How many novels have you read that didn't seem to know when to quit? The writer seemed to feel obligated to explain what happened to every character after the big event that brought everything to a close. When thinking of this problem I am always reminded of a stand-up routine Andy Griffith recorded long before he was a television star. He was pretending to be a hillbilly who had seen *Romeo and Juliet*. At the end of his recounting he said, "And seeing as how they was all dead, they brung down the curtain."

A lot of authors just don't know when to bring down the curtain.

It is sometimes necessary to provide what is called the anticlimax or dénouement, a scene which provides a tying up of loose ends. Commonly in mystery stories there was a short scene in which the sleuth explained how he or she arrived at the solution. "Elementary, my dear Watson!" On the old *Perry Mason* television series, the guilty party usually broke down in court and admitted committing the murder. That was the climax, to be promptly followed by a commercial.

After the commercial, Perry usually explained to Paul Drake or Della Street how he knew the guilty party was guilty. In romance stories there might be an anticlimax showing the couple living happily ever after. In war or historical stories, frequently we are transported to many years later, when the survivor gives us a brief summing up.

Anticlimaxes, however, should be brief. Although the information in them comes from the plot, they have little to do with the single thing that makes the plot engaging: the struggle. Anticlimaxes are afterthoughts, which may or may not add to the story. You can usually end more abruptly than you know, simply because the ending (the climax) is usually sufficient. Many beginning novelists indulge the temptation to prove they are real authors by putting a prologue at the front of their novel and an epilogue at the end, thereby beginning before the beginning and continuing after the ending. Having a prologue and an epilogue won't make you a "real writer." Usually it shows you don't know how to start or when to quit.

AMBIGUOUS ENDINGS

Another common mistake of beginning novelists is not resolving the conflict presented to the characters. The book starts fast, problems become huge, but at the point at which the ending should occur, things just taper off. Amateurs like to excuse this fundamental flaw by saying they are "leaving it up to the reader." Well, know what? The reader isn't there to write your novel. The reader is there to read your novel.

John Fowles' bestseller *The French Lieutenant's Woman* had a daring closing in which three alternative endings were offered in succession. You might call that leaving it up to the reader, but it doesn't really. The three endings are three possibilities, all offered up by the author. However, it is inevitable that the last one read will seem like the best one. If the author doesn't put the best one last, the reader will wonder why it is there at all.

The reader expects your ending to end the primary conflict, not waffle about. Yes, life's stories are often inconclusive. A suspect is caught and charged with a horrible crime. The evidence against him is rarely totally damning. Some hair and fiber, some circumstantial behavior, some partial DNA, and a myopic witness might get him the electric chair. He may get a jury of "select morons" as Raymond Chandler writes, or scrupulously honest people. His lawyer might be more interested in the publicity he's getting than working the case. Because of procedural errors the guilty verdict is appealed and a jailhouse witness comes forward who claims a now-dead inmate confessed to the crime. Is he believable or not?

This kind of thing can drag on for years and confuse anybody. In the end, we're never really sure the suspect did it, and in any case we're never really sure the punishment is justice. What punishment is adequate for those mass shootings of people who are worshipping in a church, synagogue, or mosque? Is there any way to could compensate parents for a child's death? Life doesn't give us endings as good as those in stories, but perhaps that's why we need stories. In an ideal world there would be endings. Stories function in an imaginary world. When the murderer is dragged off in chains at the end of a novel—That's all, folks! The author who fails to provide an adequate ending disappoints and irritates the audience.

A made-for-television movie I once saw provides a perfect example of the infuriating ambiguous ending. Mariette Hartly played a woman who had recently become a widow. She began dating a man, but found herself sexually attracted to a neighbor (played by Lyn Redgrave). So far, so good. The plot problem is created and then intensifies as the woman's mother and daughter are horrified by her lesbian relationship. Her boyfriend isn't too happy, either. The situation is excellent for high drama and could have been a good movie.

However, television executives have to worry about their sponsors, so coming to a resolution would have been difficult for them. They lost their nerve. If the protagonist had decided to live as a lesbian, or as a bisexual, there would have been moral outrage at that time from many groups and canceled sponsors. If she had decided to reject the lesbian life, gay rights groups would have been insulted and put pressure on sponsors. But the logic of the plot demands one of these choices. They could have copped out. Many bad stories duck a resolution in this way. They could have had her step off the curb and get flattened by a beer truck, even though something like that doesn't follow from the chain of incidents.

In an attempt to jump off the horns of their dilemma, the movie ended with the widow explaining that she was going to go off somewhere and think about her sexuality in order to make a decision some day. She wasn't sure how it would come out. As if *thinking* has anything to do with the passions! All this left viewers with, as the end titles ran, was the reaction "Huh?" This conclusion provided no resolution at all and was very unsatisfying.

THE GOD OUT OF THE MACHINE

On the other hand, some story endings are so tidy we reject them. It's rather like the cliché in mysteries in which the detective says, "I don't like it, it's just too neat." She then goes on to discover it's all a frame-up. The trouble with too-neat endings is that they appear contrived. All plots are contrived to some extent, but endings which are a bit too contrived appear unrealistic and lose their believability. In certain situations it seems impossible that everyone could live happily ever after as a conclusion to a plot. Could Elaine Robinson really run away with Benjamin after he had an affair with Elaine's mother? These characters from Charles Webb's *The Graduate* don't seem quite the Reality TV type, and the question hangs in the air. However, *The Graduate* is satirical and funny, with many exaggerated situations, so we accept this ending. In another story it wouldn't seem likely that a woman could forgive such a thing, and the ending would seem contrived.

A particular form of contrived resolution that even Aristotle criticizes in playwrights of his own time is called the *deus ex machina*, or "the god out of a machine." It seems that the actors who played gods in ancient drama were lowered from a crane or some kind of scaffold when they "came to earth." This was the machine. It was quite a bit more primitive than making Peter Pan fly in the musical, but was basically the same thing.

Mastering Plot

The objection to the god out of the machine, however, was that it was often used as a plot device. The plot began with a problem. It became more and more intense and complicated, as it should, but then the writer couldn't sort it all out. A resolution eluded him. So, the god or gods intervened like a concerned parent. "You go to your room right now!" "Kiss your sister and make up!" "Shake hands and stop fighting or I'll give you *such* a walloping!"

There is a medieval French miracle play which has the same basic plot as Shakespeare's *Merchant of Venice.* As in Shakespeare's play, the merchant borrows money from a wealthy Jew. Unlike in Shakespeare's, however, the merchant is overseas when the loan is due and casts it into the Mediterranean, trusting God to deliver it. God does, in a timely fashion, but the Jew doesn't know that the cask which floated up to his feet was from the merchant. He just thinks he's lucky. As to the merchant, the Jew demands punishment for the defaulting of the loan.

The merchant thinks he paid; the Jew thinks he didn't. They go to trial. Things are desperate. No one on earth knows the truth. But never fear! The Virgin Mary and angels appear at the trial and testify on the merchant's behalf. Naturally, this impresses the Jew and ends the disagreement. It's a perfect example of *deus ex machina* as there is no other way to resolve the problem. Shakespeare's version, of course, has the merchant go broke. A slick lawyer and a courtroom technicality (now there's realism for you!) resolve the merchant's problem

Divinity need not intervene for what we call the *deus ex machina.* Anything which is introduced at the end to resolve the central conflict, which does not logically follow from the substance of the plot, qualifies. If the surrounded wagon train in our story is down to its last box of bullets and a cavalry regiment accidentally stumbles upon the impending massacre, that's a *deus ex machina.* If the cavalry has been notified earlier in the plot and has been desperately riding to their rescue, it is not a *deus ex machina.* If the wagonmaster of the train suddenly recognizes that the enemy chief is his brother-in-law (the woman now lives on the reservation), and that ends the attack, that would be a *deus ex machina*. If we've known about the woman all along and she shoots her husband to stop the attack, that wouldn't be a *deus ex machina*. If, just as the final assault begins, there's an eclipse making the Apaches flee in terror, that's a *deus ex machina*. If the wagonmaster has been desperately holding on for three days because he knows the eclipse is coming, that's not a *deus ex machina*.

Sometimes a *deus ex machina* can be effectively used as a comic device, but even in comedy it can be risky. It requires the audience's accepting an "in" joke. *The Importance of Being Earnest* by Oscar Wilde has an ending involving the recognition of a man by means of a strawberry birthmark, but of course Wilde is making fun of the many stories in which the lost heir to the throne is recognized from a birthmark on his royal body. A certain sophistication is needed to appreciate jokes using the devices of literature, but if you like such things, you might just find an audience to laugh with you. The problem with *deus ex machina* is that it is often an invitation for the audience to laugh *at* you.

EXPECTATIONS FOR THE ENDING

What then are readers' expectations of the ending? First of all, they expect the ending to derive logically (causally, if you prefer) from the events that came before. Aristotle says that the events in a plot must have a necessary and probable relationship to one another. The ending must be a necessary and probable outcome of the chain of events that has gone before. When the readers look back over the plot, it should seem as if it could have ended in only one way. If readers refuse to accept your resolution as either being necessary or probable, they will be disappointed. They will feel you have let them down, as if you'd gone through a long joke and the punch line wasn't funny. Or, as if you'd worked out a beautiful puzzle that had no solution, a maze without an exit.

The second thing that delights readers is the unexpected. Curiously, surprises might seem to contradict the principle that the ending should derive from the plotline, but this is another of the frightening tightrope walks that all writers face. A misstep and down tumbles your plot. When the ending appears, it must seem like it had to happen, but before it appears, the readers shouldn't already know what it is going to be. When the reader can see what's coming, the story turns dull very rapidly.

Mystery fans usually play a mind game in which they try to figure out "who done it" before the detective hero. I once felt very smug at catching the essential clue in one of the Sherlock Holmes stories. Everyone in the story thought that the letters KKK were a man's initials. Instead they stood for Ku Klux Klan. Of course, Sherlock didn't grow up in the South, so I, for once, had an edge. Strangely, my pleasure was short-lived. Reading the rest of the story seemed pointless, except to confirm what I already knew. And, when, yes, I was right, I felt disappointment that my old friend Sir Arthur Conan Doyle hadn't outfoxed me.

When authors allow details to give away where the plot is going to end, they become magicians who pull the hatband out of a hat instead of rabbits. They're not very entertaining. Where's the magic in that? Sometimes we have a pretty good idea that the couple who despise each other at the beginning of s story will end up in love at the end, so the question of how this love is going to come about becomes more important than the fact they'll be in love. Nonetheless, if we seem to anticipate each move towards the inevitable conclusion, the story will be nothing but a yawner.

If stepping off the wire to the left represents the mistake of making your ending too obvious, then stepping off the wire to the right might be making your ending too outlandish. This problem is no different from failing to make strong causal connections among the successive events of the plot. Outlandish moves include introducing hitherto unmentioned characters, gadgets, or factors that only appear at the last moment. The *deus ex machina* qualifies in this regard.

Anton Chekhov, the Russian playwright and short story writer, warned that a gun hanging over a mantelpiece should be fired before the second act, but this rule cuts the other way, too. A gun fired in the second act should be in view in the first. An ending is outlandish if the cop, surrounded by thugs, suddenly "remembers" his trusty thirty-eight caliber ankle piece and mows the bad guys down. If the reader hasn't been notified of the existence of the ankle piece, it will seem like the author created it merely to get his cop out of trouble. You'll notice how regularly in good movies and books you get a glimpse of the gun in the desk drawer, long before it is used. Setting it up doesn't determine whether the gun will be used for murder, self-defense, suicide, or to crack Brazil nuts, but it creates a number of possibilities the reader might anticipate, and requires, as Chekhov said, that the gun be used somehow.

It isn't just guns, of course. You can't suddenly reveal the woman the man loves to be one of a set of identical twins. Or that the odd uncle who visits every Thanksgiving is actually a brain-sucking alien. This isn't to say you cannot have these things be your ending, but they have to meet the requirements of an ending. As ridiculous as they might seem, they must have arisen naturally (logically, causally) from the preceding material in the plot. Knowing that the man is befuddled by a set of twins would be far more enjoyable than having it sprung on a befuddled audience. (Shakespeare's *Comedy of Errors*, based on Roman playwright Plautus' *Menaechmi*, demonstrates this.) When the uncle visits every Thanksgiving, the "Thanksgiving brain-sucker" (thought to be a serial killer) claims more victims. The uncle is odd enough that the revelation of his being an alien explains that behavior.

No ending is too insane to use, as long as it is prepared for. If it isn't adequately prepared for it will always qualify as outlandish.

If your plot has begun well and risen in intensity, you have created a lot of anticipation for your ending. To let it seem too easy, too obvious, or too outlandish may disappoint your readers in a way which will destroy their positive feelings for the entire novel.

BRAINSTORMER #8

Take a novel you admire and pinpoint the central conflict. This is not always easy in certain kinds of novels.

Once you have done that, go to the back of the book and locate the precise sentence in which that conflict is resolved. This can be difficult also.

Consider how much material follows that resolution. Is there a chapter/epilogue? A bit of dialogue?

Example: Nathaniel Hawthorne's *The Scarlet Letter* can be considered a struggle for Arthur Dimmesdale's and Hester Prynne's souls. The climax is powerful. Dimmesdale dies in Hester's arms and with his last words indicates that his suffering has been rewarded with almighty forgiveness. Hawthorne follows this with a chapter of conclusion, tracing out what happened to Hester and her illegitimate child, about six book pages.

In a more modern novel, you'll usually find the resolution much closer to the last page. Elmore Leonard's *Cuba* ends with the shooting of Tavalera on page 342. The anticlimax is less than a hundred words. Bernard Malamud's *The Natural* resolves at the top of page 190 and ends on the same page.

Chapter 8
Multiple Plots

PARALLEL PLOTS

The simplest novels and many masterpieces consist of a story which runs from its beginning to its end in chronological order, but as we can see from the previous chapter there are many ways to restructure the basic plot for story purposes. Another way in which a story can be structured is for it to have what is called parallel plotting.

In the usual form of this kind of plot, the story is divided into two progressions of scenes. The chronology is preserved, so that we begin at one time and move steadily to a later one. However, we jump back and forth between two plotlines of interlinked, equal importance. The two plotlines run along next to each other (parallel) until they cross at the end. (Perhaps this type of structure shouldn't be called parallel because these non-Euclidean lines converge at the resolution of the story, but that is the common term for it. Looking down these railroad tracks they not only look like they cross, they do!)

I sometimes call the parallel plot, the "Jackal plot," because I always think of Frederick Forsyth's thriller, *The Day of the Jackal*. With apologies to the author, let me say that the summary below does not conform to Forsyth's novel, but it provides an easy way to understand parallel structuring. We have the Jackal, international terrorist, and the French policeman who wants to catch him. Antagonist and protagonist, however, will not really encounter each other until the final moment when the Jackal is about to pull the trigger to assassinate Charles De Gaulle, president of France. What we do is alternate

Mastering Plot

between what the policeman is doing to catch the Jackal and what the Jackal is doing to avoid being caught. It works as follows.

1) The policeman traces the delivery address for a rental car. When he gets there, surrounding the building with a SWAT team, the Jackal has already gone, but the car is missing.
2) The book then moves to the Jackal, who parks the car (with the keys still in the ignition) in a rundown area of Marseilles. Attacked by muggers, he kills them. The prostitute who works with them to entrap victims barely gets away.
3) The policeman arrives at Interpol in Geneva, which has recovered the car near the border. It soon becomes apparent that they have been suckered, but they find out where the car thief lived in Marseilles and connect it to the murder of two muggers.
4) The Jackal, meanwhile, tries to find the prostitute who can identify him. He tracks her to a flophouse and slits her throat from behind. He is nearly caught in the act by a group of drunk stevedores.
5) The police find out about the muggers' use of the prostitute as bait. Someone mentions the murdered woman. The Jackal mistakenly killed her roommate in the dark alley. If they can find the prostitute, they will have someone who can identify the Jackal.
6) The Jackal, unaware that a woman is alive who can identify him, is now in Morocco, buying a special sniper rifle.
5) The policeman locates the prostitute and gets an artist's rendering of the man who killed her partners in crime..

And so on. The strategy is very much like that in the silent movies in which a woman was tied to the railroad tracks. You'd see the woman struggling, then you'd see Tom Hero riding to her rescue. You'd see her panic getting worse as she hears the train, then you'd see Tom Hero galloping madly. As the story progresses, the two lines of action get closer and closer. The two main characters (whether protagonist and antagonist or hero and heroine) are moving closer to a direct encounter at the moment of highest intensity, the climax.

Sometimes in detective novels in which there are partners, such as a husband and wife, the author will parallel plot so that the husband will pursue the clues in his own way while simultaneously the wife will pursue clues in her own, very different way. Each thinks the other's method is ridiculous. They, of course, end up at the same place, bumping into each other in astonishment. "What are *you* doing here?" he says. "Shush! I hear someone coming!" she says.

Parallel plotting requires that the two story lines be roughly equal in interest and importance to the outcome of the struggle. If the reader senses that one of them is less important or interesting, or that it doesn't sufficiently illuminate the plot it is parallel with, he or she may begin to skip the weaker plot sections, and you will have lost them.

Many books may use the parallel plot strategy for the entire book. That can be very symmetrical and admirable technique. But never let technique alone tell you how to write. Do not sustain parallel plotting if you cannot make the separate threads equally compelling. You don't want your reader admiring your technique (most won't give a fig about technique), but feeling indifferent to the problems and emotions you are portraying. The reason you're learning about technique is to better communicate feelings.

For this reason, novels which use parallel plots often use them for only part of the book. As we mentioned, it is a very attractive strategy for pursuits of any kind. The French policeman pursues the Jackal. Love stories are sometimes pursuits, and it is easy to imagine a plot cutting back and forth between the Jack and his Jill. In many books the pursuit is not the entire book, however, so paralleling occurs as only a part of the entire book.

In *The Silence of the Lambs*, for example, most of the book follows Clarice Starling, the young FBI agent. Thomas Harris (the author), however, breaks away occasionally to other characters, such as when he portrays the sad personal life of Clarice's supervisor Jack

Mastering Plot

Crawford. The parallel plot, however, is that of Buffalo Bill, the psycho, who is trying to fatten up his captive in a way that would make her suitable to skin. The captive resists, of course, but only Clarice who can save her, and the clock is running.

This fattening up business, however, isn't very interesting, so most of what we see is Clarice trying to get clues from Hannibal Lecter and others. Until the end, that is. The danger is more imminent. Buffalo Bill may get to his hideous work at any moment, so there is a lot of jumping back and forth. Harris also adds a third parallel line which enhances the excitement immensely. Crawford and the other FBI agents have identified what they think is Buffalo Bill's house. They are closing in with a SWAT team which may be needed to save Clarice, who has already gone inside. They are coming like the cavalry in an old western to save her from a danger she doesn't know exists. But they don't know she's there, and she doesn't know they are coming.

The great trick of this is, of course, that the cavalry is going to the wrong place. Their plotline ends in a dead-end, a charge into an empty house. Clarice is now utterly alone, on her way to a direct encounter with Buffalo Bill in the dark basement. The plotlines meet in their struggle.

POINT OF VIEW

Writing parallel plots obviously also requires attention to another aspect of novel writing, one I feel is sometimes belabored. Obviously, parallel plotlines require either an omniscient point of view or multiple points of view. Usually the latter is what is used. The omniscient point of view, in which the author is allowed to range from mind to mind in various characters is still in use, but is often considered Victorian and feels a bit odd. Since the 1920s, readers are more used to limited points of view in which we see a scene through the eyes of only one character. We are given only that single character's interpretation of what is going on. Even if a book is full of characters, usually we experience each scene through the eyes of only one of them. In a novel which contains the simplest kind of parallel plotting, we will jump from one point of view to a second point of view, and then back to the first.

If we were, for example, to have parallel plots in a novel involving protagonist Joe Worldsaver and antagonist Lionel Terrorist, we would perhaps begin with a scene in which Joe gets a taunting letter from Lionel, who is threatening to poison Lake Michigan. Joe reads the letter and tries to decide what to do. Then, we would jump to the parallel plot, and see that Lionel is murdering the guy who carried the letter for him. Lionel's letter is really a trick to distract Joe from Lake Superior. You can see how this creates a new tension. The reader knows what Joe doesn't. How will Joe find out he's being deceived, or will it be too late? There are many ways of handling point of view, which we don't need to go into here. You could, for instance, write from a very detached point of view, a camera view, in which you don't go into any character's mind, but only show them in action.

This point of view business can be quite tricky in particular ways which you need to watch for. Remember that each line of a parallel plot should hold approximately the same level of interest. However, a different point of view requires a different way of looking at things and the differences of language you would expect from different characters. Joe doesn't think the same as Lionel; Lionel has a different vocabulary than Joe. When you switch from plotline to plotline, readers should not be confused as to which plotline they are in. They should be different in language and tone, but (usually) not so different that it seems you're trying to be clever. The difference should seem natural, not forced.

It gets particularly tricky when you have two characters in parallel plotlines who should be similar in language, etc., because of who they are. Would we believe two sisters with radically different dialects? Twins who have radically different vocabularies? It makes sense that two guys who grow up on the same block might use the same expressions, unless there is another factor: one goes to college; the other doesn't. These are largely matters of characterization, of course, but if you choose to use parallel plots, you might need to address such problems.

Another problem which can arise in using parallel plots is that of chronology. Although you have two (or more) plotlines, they do not operate independently. Each is part of the other and affects the other. Thus, they are not really two plots, but one. The chronological progression we expect in a single plot would also be expected in parallel plots. The novel must move forward. A common mistake of people trying out parallel plotting is that they repeat the time frames too regularly.

Let me explain. Suppose the first passage in which we see Joe takes place on a Wednesday from three to four in the afternoon. The next passage, featuring Lionel, takes place on a Wednesday from three to four in the afternoon. In itself, this isn't a great problem if there is substantially different information in the Lionel passage. However, the constant motion of going forward to come back to go forward to the same point can quickly become tiresome. It slows down the sense of forward motion.

In the A. Alvarez novel *Day of Atonement*, a husband and wife, Joe and Judy Constantine, are the two main narrators. Oftentimes the main point of a passage is that Joe sees things very differently from Judy, although they are both undergoing stress to their marriage and a severe threat from gangsters. However, Alvarez does a very simple thing which keeps the energy of novel moving forward. He does not repeat very much. Joe tells what happened. The wife picks up the story at the point in time where he left off. In this way Alvarez interestingly represents the different perceptions of this couple, but also wisely keeps the novel progressing instead of jerking back and forth.

THE SUBPLOT

Another form of multiple plotting is called the subplot. A subplot is similar to a parallel plot; however, it is not equal to it in intensity. *Sub* is Latin for "under" or "lower," as in submarine ("under the sea") and "subordinate" ("of a lower order or rank"). A subplot is, therefore, an "under-plot" or "a plot of a lower order." It is a secondary plot which operates within the context of a story, but which is not as important to the story as the primary plot. It could not exist independently and be as powerful.

In a number of historical novels we find the following plot scheme. There is a noble man who loves a noble woman. There is, however, an obstacle to their becoming husband and wife. The main movement of the novel is about their overcoming the obstacles to be together. Similar to the main plot, however, is a subplot in which the servant of the noble man takes a liking to the noble woman's maidservant. In the happy ending, they, too, wind up being a couple, though they could not if the noble couple did not hook up.

In such novels, often there are many contrasts between the high-society and low-society couples. The nobles are young, handsome and beautiful. They dress nicely. They have the highest motivations and behave impeccably. The poetry of their language speaks to their fine breeding. The servants, however, speak anything but poetry. There may be more lechery than love in their passion. They dress like, well, servants. Their teeth may be crooked and they may be quite unattractive and much older than their superiors.

The subplot of the servingman seeking the servingwoman often functions as comic relief to the main plot. When the emotion gets too intense, comic relief allows the audience off the hook for a moment, so that all that intensity doesn't burn them out. Victor Hugo once remarked that Shakespeare often used comedy to make tragedy seem more tragic and sadness to make comedy seem more comic. We can see this in *Macbeth*. There is the tension of the first act, building and building. Will Macbeth give in to all the pressures and murder King Duncan? The witches tease him; Lady Macbeth pushes him. Finally in a great explosion of madness and blood, the deed is done. What is the next scene? Not another one of higher intensity. How high can we get?

No, it is the porter at the door we see next. A dirty man, drunk out of his head, makes jokes as he tries to gather himself to answer the pounding at the door. It is anything but tragic. But what it does is to let the audience relax. After this scene the intensity can begin to rise again, until we reach more madness and blood: Macbeth's severed head on a pole.

The porter, however, is not part of a subplot. He serves his purpose as comic relief and then moves on. Our example of the servants consists of a continuing story which counterpoints the main story. Different parts of the subplot can act as comic relief, but there is a causal chain connecting the different parts, just as in a typical plot, even though the subplot is not as intense as the primary plot. Or perhaps we should say it is not the audience's focus of attention as much as the primary plot.

The subplot is a fraternal twin to the main plot, but not an identical twin. It is related, but not a duplicate. In the film of James Michener's novel *Sayonara*, an Air Force major, Lloyd Gruver (played by Marlon Brando) is stationed in postwar Japan. In a way that parallels the nobles-and-servants plot we discussed earlier, Gruver is from a good family, has big prospects, and is expected to marry a general's daughter. However, he falls in love with a Japanese theater performer, Hana-ogi. In one subplot, Airman Joe Kelly also falls in love with a Japanese woman, but the military doesn't allow him to marry. He deserts and commits suicide with the woman he loves. The officer is affected by his sergeant's death and follows his heart, giving up everything to be with Hana-ogi.

The parallels between the two plots are the men's falling in love, the racial prejudices they face, and the institutional hurdles designed to protect soldiers in foreign lands from acting too hastily when it comes to marrying the natives. The results of the men's actions are, however, very different. While the sergeant's actions are understandable, he doesn't have the patience and strength of the officer, ending up dead as a result. The officer, who might be strong enough to set aside his love for Hana-ogi, learns from his sergeant's experience. He is sickened by the evil results of prejudice, and sees the supremacy of love over material things. This gives him the additional strength to do the right thing, which is to run into the arms of Hana-ogi.

From this example you can see that the story of the sergeant and his love has all of the qualities of a main plot. It has conflict and a chronological progression of causally linked events. With some embellishment and elaboration, it could be the main plot of a novel. However, it is used here to highlight the issues raised by the main plot and to influence the direction of it.

SUBPLOTTING FOR ITS OWN SAKE

A subplot should never be irrelevant to the main plot. It should enhance and enrich the main plot. It should also never be a mere repetition of the main plot, but by its similarities and contrasts with the main plot clarify the issues of the main plot.

Sometimes writers get a little bored with their plot or begin to think it is a too thin to carry the full weight of a novel. And they are often right in thinking so. But they are afraid to face the fact that their plot might be better as a short story or that horrible-to-sell thing we call a novella—too long for a magazine and too short for a book. Instead of beefing up their main plot, they resort to a subplot to pad out the book. In such an instance, if the subplot is not naturally relevant to the main plot, it becomes an odd appendage, glued onto the story like a clock stuck into the belly of a Venus de Milo.

I recall teaching a novel in which a subplot involving love letters from a soldier overseas was interwoven with a mystery story. Chapters would alternate with short chapters containing the letters, like this ("L" representing the letters):

A----L1----B----L2----C----L3 and so on.

There was a subplot in the letters about the character trying to survive the war to get back to his girl as the war scarred and changed him. The main plot (A, B, C, etc.) was about a woman being stalked by an unknown killer. Later in the book we find out that the killer was influenced by reading the letters. He was trying in some warped way to avenge his older brother's death in the war, blaming it on the woman who got tired of waiting for her boyfriend to come home.

The subplot in the letters was, therefore, related to the main plot, but a little too loosely. They could not affect the main plot because they were twenty years old and no one in the main plot was aware of them, other than the killer. The effect they had on the killer had already taken place when the first stalking incident took place at the beginning. The warping of the killer was, therefore, not taking place in the letters or along the same time line as the stalking plot. We learned a lot about a character who had been dead for twenty years and who only appeared in the main plot as a memory, or a photograph.

The subplot plainly didn't work. My students (an intelligent bunch) admitted they had soon recognized that the letters (printed in italics) weren't going to tell them who the stalker was. They were interested in the woman being stalked, the policeman who was trying to protect her, and all of the usual suspects. After about five letters, my students confessed, they saw italics and skipped to where the italics ended, to where the "real novel" was. They felt annoyed that so much of the book had been filled with a subplot that did not illuminate—in any significant way—the main plot. With half the book skipped over, the main plot that was left then seemed very slight. It could have been beefed up and expanded in those wasted italicized pages. Should I have chastised my students for failing to read the whole book? Not when I myself had skipped the letters, too.

THE 200-POUND SUBPLOT

Another thing which can go wrong with a subplot: it begins to dominate the main plot. We want all of our novels to be as interesting as possible, but we've got to concentrate on the movement of the primary plot. There have been some scholars who have argued that what happens in Shakespeare's *Much Ado About Nothing* is an example of a comic subplot overwhelming the main plot. Basically, it is a typical Shakespearean comedy in which young people pair off and after considerable confusion end up in a frenzy of marrying. The couple that is vividly remembered from *Much Ado* is that of Beatrice and Benedick. These are the plum parts for actors appearing in that play.

However, the main plot concerns the lovers Claudio and Hero. Because of the evil deceptions of Don John, the bastard brother of the Prince of Aragon, Claudio rejects Hero at the altar and the whole main story comes near to a tragedy. Only another deception saves their marriage. Claudio comes across as undeserving of Hero in all this. His willingness to believe Don John's tricks and his meanspirited behavior when he believes Hero to have cheated on him, makes us doubt the depth of his love. Compared to Benedick, he's also a bore. Compared to Beatrice, Hero is as interesting as an innocent victim usually is—about as exciting as the first character killed in a horror movie.

Beatrice and Benedick fight each other constantly. They have wonderful battles of wit. When their characters are on stage we expect and receive fireworks and fun. It is much more interesting to watch this couple come to realize their love for one another, than it is to watch Claudio get a woman he doesn't quite deserve. Yet, Beatrice and Benedick's plot is clearly the subplot. The consequence of their love story is not as significant as Claudio and Hero's, which threatens to lead to a death. It is the comic counterpoint to the main plot. It reflects the main plot in its use of deception. While Benedick is being deceived by Claudio, Claudio is the victim of Don John. What he gives, in other words, he gets back with interest, deserving the suffering that comes his way.

It isn't easy to say that Shakespeare goofed this up. But *Much Ado* is a troublesome play, at least partly because of this structural flaw in which the subplot is more compelling than the main plot.

Another interesting example of this flaw is in the otherwise excellent novel by Thomas Harris, *The Silence of the Lambs*. Harris' main plot runs as follows. "Buffalo Bill," a serial killer, has kidnapped the daughter of a senator. There is practically nothing to go on, but a maniac (Hannibal Lecter) incarcerated in a Maryland hospital for the criminally insane might know something helpful. Young FBI agent Clarice Starling is sent to interview Lecter to get whatever crumbs of clues she can. He has no reason to help, being such a dangerous criminal that he will never be released. Starling and Lecter engage in a lot of wordplay, but for unknown reasons, Lecter plays along, giving hints to Starling, and manipulating her. These hints lead to Buffalo Bill. Clarice confronts him alone, barely escaping with her life, but rescuing the senator's daughter.

So, what is wrong with this? The main plot pits the protagonist Starling against Buffalo Bill. Lecter is an obstacle on her way to rescuing the senator's daughter and stopping Buffalo Bill. Bill, however, is just a psycho. He never quite seems a worthy adversary, though he is a dangerous one in the dark in his basement. There isn't much more to running him to ground than what we've seen in dozens of thrillers. Hannibal Lecter is much more interesting, and the subplot of his using Starling to escape confinement is incredibly memorable. In the book, the mental cat and mouse game between Lecter and Starling is electrifying, although both characters are sitting still much of the time. Lecter's power carried over into the motion picture. It earned Anthony Hopkins an Academy Award for portraying the madman, even though Lecter is, in terms of plot structure, a secondary character. When the opportunity for a sequel to *Silence of the Lambs* came along, Lecter was required to be in it. He was promoted a primary character, and *Hannibal* became the book's title.

Perhaps at this point in the discussion you will think, "I wish I could have as many flaws as Harris and Shakespeare." However, it isn't the flaws that make these stories compelling, it is their other considerable assets, assets so powerful that they make us willing to forgive the flaws. *Much Ado* is a classic, but it is a long way from Shakespeare's best. *Silence of the Lambs* really is an excellent page turner, but that doesn't mean it's structurally perfect.

In less effective stories, the subplot dominating the main plot merely points up how uninteresting the main plot is, and makes it seem even duller by contrast. It kills the whole story as the reader doesn't know what to focus on.

What do you do if you find your subplot dominating your plot? What would you do if you found out your second-string first baseman was a better hitter than your first-string baseman? You swap them. You'd send the former first-stringer down to the minors or retire him. A good team manager wouldn't hesitate.

Reconsider your novel. What would your novel be like if the subplot became the main plot? Often a subplot (even if its more interesting) doesn't have enough going on to be a main plot. You might need to beef it up. Often the characters in a subplot lack the depth of the characters you've created for the main plot. If you want to "promote" the subplot to main plot, you might have to change sidekicks into protagonists with the multiple dimensions of character that a sidekick doesn't need. The sidekick might change so drastically, he or she is not the same at all. Instead of a lovable Thelma Ritter/Gabby Hayes kind of flat character, you'll have someone with a past, parents, traumas, a bank account, and so forth. In writing, there are always a million things to consider when making a change.

EPISODIC PLOTTING

Sportswriters are faced with a difficult problem similar to that faced by many novelists. Sports stories are basically the same week after week. In major league baseball, they now play 164 games a year, and then the play-offs. What happens on one day is pretty much the same as what happened the previous. One team won and another team lost. To add interest, flamboyant verbs and metaphors are common. Four Notre Dame players were famously compared to the Four Horseman of the Apocalypse by Grantland Rice. The word "immortal" is bandied about. When reading a string of scores, announcers say "pounded," "thumped," "outlasted," "hung on to beat," "annihilated," and other such overstatements. But all this diction isn't enough to elevate what amounts to a list of numbers.

The nagging feeling that sports isn't really very important also leads the writers to place it in heroic and legendary contexts. The need for a larger story leads to such on-running tales as the quest for the championship, the quest for the Heisman, the home run race, or the long list of records (many of them not very significant) which fall every year. Though each game takes place independently, it is linked to other games by the imposition of a much longer, and supposedly more significant, story, such as Harvard's century of playing Yale, or the history of games played in a soon-to-be dismantled stadium. Each episode (game) is a conflict in itself, which is interesting in and of itself, but a game cannot last a whole sporting season.

Similarly, for novelists there is a loose variety of plot, commonly called episodic. It consists of discrete units, little stories in themselves, which are part of a larger story. The causal chain from episode to episode is not as tight as it is in non-episodic plots. To be successful, each episode must create its own interest and be somewhat connected to the other episodes. Episodes must not seem repetitive, or the book can become tedious. Ideally, also, there is an increase in intensity, so that the importance of episodes build from the first to the last, which should seem more important than any which came before.

Although Aristotle tells us the episodic plot is inferior to the non-episodic plot, many of literature's greatest works are episodic. Voltaire's *Candide*, Cervantes' *Don Quixote*, Rabelais' *Gargantua and Pantagruel*, *The Thousand and One Arabian Nights*, and *The Odyssey* (as Aristotle points out) are all episodic. The main characters go through a series of adventures, each of which can be interesting in itself. Each episode has the structure of a plot, beginning with a problem and progressing through to a climax.

In *The Odyssey*, for example, Odysseus lands on the island of the one-eyed giants, the Cyclops. One Cyclops manages to imprison Odysseus and his men and to eat several of them. Odysseus sharpens a pole in the fire, tells the Cyclops his name is Nobody, and stabs the pole into the Cyclops' eye. The other Cyclops hear him screaming, but when they shout "What is wrong?" he answers that Nobody has hurt him. Odysseus then manages to escape. The episode stands alone as a good story in itself and can be presented without the context of Odysseus' ten year voyage home. The episode has a plot, beginning with a problem of great seriousness which rises in intensity and ends with the resolution of that problem.

Aristotle criticizes plots which are unified only by the fact that the same character is the subject of each episode. He writes of ancient authors who composed epics or dramas based on events in the life of Heracles or other heroes. However, Aristotle does not say *The Odyssey* is a failure for being episodic, only that its structure is weaker than that of *The Iliad.* The latter has many digressions, such as the famous "catalog of ships," a long passage of great interest to scholars, which lists all of the allies in the Greek cause. However, *The Iliad* remains one complete plot concerning the anger of Achilles and the consequences of it. *The Odyssey*, as a whole, tells the story of Odysseus' quest to return home after the war. However, it tells the story through a series of episodes, which (as I've said) can stand alone. The final episode, his return and retaking control of his kingdom, works as a resolution to his larger problem of getting home. Yet, it, too, could stand alone. Even if he had lived like Robinson Crusoe on a desert island without an adventure during the entire ten years in which he encountered the Lotus eaters, the Cyclops, Calypso, and so on, the final episode would not be appreciably different. A slight change in the events of *The Iliad*, however, would more likely change the resolution as well. *The Iliad* is a line of dominoes which fall in order from one end to the other. *The Odyssey* is more like groups of dominoes which have to be restarted at intervals.

The Iliad and *The Odyssey* are convenient examples, even if they are not novels, because they were allegedly written by the same author. Besides the novels mentioned above, we might also include *David Copperfield*, *Tom Sawyer*, *Gulliver's Travels*, *The Painted Bird* by Jerzy Kosinski, *Good Soldier Schweik* by Jaroslav Hasek, *Roots* by Alex Haley, *The Secret Pilgrim* by John Le Carré, and many others. Episodic structure has been particularly successful in stories which have a strong element of the journey in them. In *Gulliver's Travels* and *The Odyssey*, the journey is an obvious physical one. In others, the emphasis is more on a spiritual or mental journey. *The Secret Pilgrim* by John Le Carré is a collection of reminiscences by a retiring spy. Usually, however, there are elements of both. How can a character undertake a physical journey without also changing internally?

Episodic plotting is also used by authors who intend to create a panoramic view of a nation or a society. *Airport* by Arthur Hailey gives us the stories of a number of individuals at different levels of society, all brought together in the context of the airport. This is perhaps closer to parallel plotting, but it is possible to imagine a number of these individuals removed from the book with little effect. John Dos Passo's trilogy of novels, *U.S.A.*, is deliberately episodic to show the many facets of life in the United States. Emile Zola's *Germinal* is the story of a coal miners' strike, but by comparing scenes of the miners' lives with scenes of the managers' and owners' lives, Zola creates an overview of the situation. His treatment, like Hailey's, could be looked upon as parallel plotting, but it sometimes has an episodic quality.

We might look on the episodic quality in plotting as ranging over a spectrum. At one end we have the totally integrated plot with a tight causal chain. We move across the spectrum then to episodes which are related by time or character, but not as tightly related by cause and effect. At the extreme other end, we might have not a novel, but a collection of short stories loosely related by place or character, such as Sherwood Anderson's *Winesburg, Ohio* or even Geoffrey Chaucer's *The Canterbury Tales*. In the latter case, the stories are so loosely connected that they do not build the book to a resolution, but rather build by accumulation of story on top of story. This accumulated effect would not, however, create what would normally be called a novel. A novel requires a greater unity of plot. Identifying exactly where a novel structure ceases to be "episodic" and becomes a cycle of related stories is a matter of perception. However, if a set of stories is unified only by setting and the protagonists vary from episode to episode we would almost always say the book is a collection of short stories rather than a loose novel.

For some beginning writers, the panorama and multiple characters of the episodic novel is very attractive. It seems like more fun to write. It even seems easier. The long grind of working on the same storyline for months sounds boring by comparison. Instead of making a great single-flavor soup, such as French onion or mulligatawny, we'll make pease porridge and throw in whatever we have in the fridge, letting the flavor come as it may. Yet, writing a *good* episodic novel has its own difficulties. Each episode in the novel has to have its own interest, so the writer has to begin again with each episode, carrying over the protagonist, perhaps, but presenting her or him with a new problem and situation. Instead of a chapter or scene springing from the conclusion of the previous, the writer is almost beginning over again at each episode. Each episode much have some consistency with the others, yet not become repetitive. And all of this must take place within a general sense by the reader that the episodes are leading somewhere, ideally that they are building up to an ending as boffo climactic as the slaying of the suitors in *The Odyssey*.

No, writing in episodes is not the easy way out. Regardless of how much fun—addicting!—writing a novel can be, it is never easy. Each form has its own particular difficulties which the writer must face.

BRAINSTORMER #9

Select one of your favorite novels. Decide whether it uses parallel plots, subplots, or episode plotting. If it doesn't and it's the genre of novel you want to write, keep that in mind, as it might be one of the patterns in your genre. But if it doesn't have parallel plots, subplots or episode plotting, confirm the pattern by selecting another of the same genre and see if the pattern is consistent.

If, on the other hand, the novel you've selected has either parallel plots or subplots, chart their progress through the book in the way that was represented previously: A is the main plot, B is a parallel plot to

A. Subplots can be represented by lower case letters. You might end up with something like this:

A–B–A–Ba–A–A–a–B–B–A–ABa

That last chapter would be quite an accomplishment, not only do the parallel plots combine with each other, the subplot to the A plot gets into it.

If you discover that the novel you've selected has an episodic plot, charting it out won't be particular helpful. However, notice the length and number of episodes. Are episodes roughly of the same length? Do they cover similar amounts of time? Are they in chronological order or do they jump backwards and forwards?

Finally, pay particular attention as to the methods by which the author achieves unity in an episodic plot. Does the novel focus on the journeys of a single character? Does it set up a situation which allows for a unity based on a group of people (such as pilgrims going to Canterbury)? In short, how does the author keep the episodes as part of a novel rather than a collection of short stories?

When you go to plot out your book, keep your analyses of other novels in mind and try to keep your structure as simple as possible in order to tell the kind of story you are trying to tell. You will undoubtedly find novels written by others that use complex structures to cover up the fact they have little to say. Remember that and never complicate your plot structure merely because it seems "arty" to do so. Model your books on the most effective plots, not the fanciest.

Chapter 9
Integrating Character And Plot

The second most important element in a novel, character, is much more a matter of shading and subtlety than is plot. A plot is a structure that must be sturdy, logical, and well-constructed to achieve its best effects. Character, being a simulation of people, must exhibit the strange mixture of consistency and inconsistency that people exhibit.

If we go back to our architectural metaphors, the plot is the framing that holds up a wall. Many kinds of walls can be placed on the framing. Drywall, plaster and lathe, brick, plywood, tar paper, planking, bead board are all common. We might imagine a very long list of wall treatments, some revolting and others boring, but it would be relatively short compared to all the variety of characters we might create. Lawrence Block once entitled a novel *Eight Million Ways to Die* referring to the number of inhabitants of New York City. Each person lives and dies in a different way.

This is not to say that most walls aren't drywall covered with Sears flat white. Yes, people can be numbingly similar, or at least so numbingly unsurprising that they would make good characters in a novel if their ordinariness is all the author concentrated on. Examined closely, however, even cans of flat white latex have differences, and a few weeks of being on the wall allows that color to be affected by sunlight, dampness, children with their crayons, and the scratches made by moving furniture. Part of the measure of your skill as a novelist will consist of how well you can recognize the differences among very similar characters and how you can make the reader see the uniqueness of each of your characters.

There is no alarm bell that goes off louder in my head than when an aspiring author describes one of his or her characters as "typical." *Forget typical.* No real person is typical. You're not "typical" are you? Shoot! You want to write a novel! There's nothing typical about that. If you're trying to improve a novel you've already written, you're unusual in having actually completed a manuscript. Don't feel superior and say, "Well, yes, I'm unusual, but most people..." If you feel that way, you have no place in the novel business. You haven't looked closely enough at your fellow human beings. Jane Goodall and other scientists who have lived closely among chimpanzees and gorillas soon find differences of personality and temperament among our primate cousins. If you can't see such differences among people, you're not going to be much of a fiction writer.

"Average" is a mathematical concept and the lie of it is shown in statistics which tell us the typical family has 1.62 children. Exactly what 0.38 part of the second child is left off? Little Debbie lacks a head? It is easy for pollsters and newscasters to generalize with such figures. So many million people own computers. So many people wish they had more attractive features. So many are obese and so many believe in God and so many are opposed to intervention in East Timor. This is not to say that demographics is not useful in certain fields at certain times, but that they don't really tell us much about individuals.

Why does Harry G. weigh 300 pounds and Elmore D. weigh 750? Both are obese. How has it affected the way each looks at life? Is one offensive and crude in his speech, the other surprisingly gentle and mannered? Two women grow up in the same small town in Indiana, dress much alike, and were both raised in the Second Church of Saintly Futures. Eliza T. answers the phone poll and says she believes in God. Emma G. answers the same. What kind of God does each believe in? How much does this belief affect their individual behaviors? Eliza thinks God will punish her for doing certain things, even though she goes ahead and does them. Does she want to be punished? Emma thinks God forgives everything, and happily sins while Eliza ruefully sins.

Let's repeat the concept: No one is typical. And just as no two human being are alike, no two characters can be alike. Characters that are typical are phony. They are doomed to be uninteresting because the reader immediately knows they are phony. Their resemblance to life is insufficient. They are not lifelike.

Besides being lifelike and consistent, Aristotle mentions two other qualities which character should possess. One is appropriateness. He uses horribly inappropriate examples for this, which are woefully outdated, saying that a female character should not be "manly" or "clever." But that doesn't mean his basic principle is flawed. It wouldn't be appropriate for a character who is six foot six and two hundred and ninety pounds to be a jockey. Readers would find that ridiculous. A character who grew up on a farm in the Ozarks who has a British accent would also be laughable.

People are interesting mixtures. I had an uncle who had suffered brain damage in his childhood, but who could tell you the exact date and day on which every member of our large extended family was born, married, and died. It is not inappropriate, given the well-documented "idiot savant" syndrome, that he should be utterly inadequate on the SATs but have such a phenomenal memory for dates.

Another of the qualities which Aristotle says a character should have is goodness. Obviously, he must be referring to the main character and we need to remember that Aristotle was writing of a type of drama that was also religious ritual. To Aristotle, morality is an important aspect to drama. I think it is, too, but in a slightly different way. Each story implies values and even if writers are striving for "pure entertainment," they will always imply that one thing is good and another evil. The best writers point out the fuzzy areas between good and evil. What makes *The Caine Mutiny* by Herman Wouk so interesting at the end is not that Captain Queeg is proven incompetent and the young officers' careers are saved. It is the moment when their attorney takes the story one step further and makes the officers see that perhaps they could have handled it all better, that Queeg deserved better than they gave him.

When we present a main character, however, we must make the reader sympathize or identify with him or her. In a sense, we must believe the protagonist is "good." Otherwise, we won't care what happens. It is repulsive to see good person brought down by a bad person. This angers us. A plot may lead to the defeat of a good person, but if it is a sacrifice or a tragedy, the good person is only physically defeated, not spiritually. When Gunga Din in Kipling's poem warns the troops and dies preventing the surprise attack, he becomes, in the words of the narrator, "a better man than I am." In the *Chanson de Roland*, Roland saves Christendom in a similar manner, by blowing a horn to summon King Charles, but he, also, is killed by the enemy.

As many commentators have pointed out, the end of a tragedy almost always creates an uplifting feeling. Though Oedipus wanders off the stage blinded, though Hamlet lies dead and Willie Loman of *The Death of a Salesman* has died, each has taken all that a cruel universe can dish out and transcended it, creating meaning by their suffering.

Modern writers get nervous at the word "good," thinking of preachy and goody-two-shoes fiction, but even the most outrageous anti-hero must create a feeling of identification in the audience. We delight in the successful con man character, as long as he is fleecing bad guys. We make heroes of bank robbers and train robbers, as long as they do it out of a Robin Hood motive or because the bankers or the railroad moguls are more evil.

Sometimes we enjoy the way a character defies all the conventions of a corrupt or phony society. The heroes of the film *Easy Rider* and the protagonist of the novel, *A Confederacy of Dunces*, all do this. When the Marx Brothers are throwing potatoes at a fancy-dress ceremonial occasion, they are doing this, too, and we love it. None of these people are "good" in the conventional sense, though we sympathize with them because we wish we had the courage to make the choices they make.

Often, we find characters who are obviously not good, yet are occupying the protagonists role and we are fascinated by them. Chief among them is Shakespeare's Richard III, who lets us know from the beginning of the play that he intends to use every evil trick in the book to get himself the crown. He is deformed and the people around him often get what they deserve, but it is difficult to say we sympathize with a character who brings about the murder of two children. He is witty and clever, but it would be a stretch to say that we admire him. He has courage and dies well in the end, but it's hardly for a noble cause. Good is just not the word for this devil, though he is fascinating as a devil. More recently the example of Hannibal Lecter might be cited, though he is not really the protagonist of *The Silence of the Lambs*. Somehow, despite our revulsion for the acts of such characters, an author can make us identify with them, to understand their mad reasoning and be interested in where it will lead. This works in a way similar to the way we identify with good characters.

So, then, a character must be lifelike—that is, unique and yet recognizable as within the limits of appropriate behavior. It must be consistent, not outlandishly changing from page to page. Finally, and perhaps most importantly, a character must engage the readers enough to make them care about what happens to it.

This is not a book about creating characters, however. I've just gone through the basics in order to create a basis for our real question. How does plotting relate to achieving effective characterization?

DEEDS, NOT WORDS

As I said early in this book, you can only know the character of a person by what he or she does. In moments of duress, people react. Their reactions tell you what their inner natures, or characters, are.

Let me tell you a true story. I had just finished lecturing to a very large class and was speaking with a woman (let's call her Patty) who was writing a senior thesis. After a few seconds, there was no one left in the room but me, her, and a young man who was still sitting at his desk. It was such a large class that I recognized him, but couldn't recall his name. He suddenly threw a notebook across the empty seats. I asked him if I could help him with something. He didn't answer. I thought perhaps he was angry about something, perhaps exasperated with the difficulty of college life. But he said nothing, so I continued to talk with Patty.

Suddenly, he strolled down the side aisle to the corner and raised the overhead projector off its cart, heaving it at us. The projector crashed to the floor. Glass splintered and flew everywhere. If the thing had struck either of us we could have been injured, even killed. Patty retained her sense of decent language and said something like "What are you doing?!" I said something quite a bit more colorful (something my father would have said), but I won't repeat here.

The young man then assumed a martial arts stance and said something to the effect that he was going to kick my posterior. I asked him if he was high on something. He repeated his threat. I was continuing to back away from this glassy-eyed boy, not sure he couldn't kick my untrained posterior, when he suddenly leapt at Patty. Something went off in my head. Something of my Virginia upbringing. I didn't say it, but it was a kind of Southern thing: "Unhand that woman!" I grabbed him, pulled him away from her and entangled the boy's arms.

As she went for the police, the boy got away and kicked at me. He barely missed and I instantly knocked him to the floor. He fell hard, but moved to get up until I stood over him. I looked him straight in the eye and snarled, "If you get up, I'll hurt you!" To my astonishment, that seemed to intimidate him until the police arrived. When they did, he threatened them, spat on one officer, and was rewarded with being thrown again to the floor, handcuffed, and sat on.

The policewoman searched his pockets for drugs and found an old, beaten-up joint in his wallet, but knew this behavior wasn't just marijuana. The boy was diabetic. It occasionally happens that when the blood sugar goes awry, that weird behavior results. The officer pumped glucose in his mouth and in a few moments he was asking what had happened. I had never heard of this phenomenon, but later I noticed that his seat was covered with snack food wrappers. He had felt the attack coming on and had quickly eaten chips and crackers trying to ward it off.

I was very grateful his temporary madness extended to attacking the police. At least it could no longer be just his word against Patty's and mine. In the end, the police did nothing about the joint, the school didn't bill him for the overhead projector, and the boy sheepishly completed the class.

This was an extraordinary moment of duress, and quite a lesson to me about who I am. The last time I had fought anyone, it was over his breaking my plastic Army helmet with his plastic rifle. I never played football, boxed, or studied tae kwon do, so had no real training to deal with violence. Yet, when this incredibly weird episode happened I discovered these things in myself I never knew were there. I flew to Patty's defense without hesitation or thought. Yet, I was never angry at the boy. I never felt the kind of fury I would have assumed would go with it. My threat to hurt him, I know, was serious, though the wording has an awful B-movie sound to it—probably the result of misspent hours in front of the tube. I was ready to hurt him at the same time I was thinking that the situation was absurd, that the administration would throw a professor to the dogs for this. The wingbeats of vulture-like attorneys with career-ending lawsuits were nearly audible.

I never imagined that I would be able to have coherent thoughts while something like this happened. I never knew that I would be so capable of maintaining my cool. I saw aspects of my father coming out in what I had said and done, things I knew were in him, but did not know I had absorbed. He was revolted by a man striking a woman and would have interfered in such a circumstance. He had boxed. He had played football. He once fought a man in an alley who had tried to rob him. But I was a bookish boy, with glasses the thickness of English muffins, who outran trouble rather than confronting it.

Compared to me, however, the police officers were sleep walking. When they realized they were going to have to use physical force to subdue the boy, the cop actually sighed before flying into instant, ruthless action. In his sigh, you could hear a kind of boredom. Oh, well, here we go again . . . . And yet they had the glucose in their car for exactly such an eventuality, they gave the boy a pass on the joint, and did not charge him for assaulting a police officer. They acted with the highest professionalism and common sense.

What is the point of this story? As I recounted the events to you, didn't various understandings of the people involved begin to gel? As I learned about myself, you received hints about who I am. As I understood the police officers better, you did, too. What each of us did in that stressful situation revealed something about us. Under stress, the mask drops. You act, or you don't act. It doesn't matter which. To refuse to decide something is to have made a decision to refuse. Either way, you have created an impression of what potentials exist within you.

In the realm of story, as in the realm of life, events and the reaction to them tell us who a character is. In the early twentieth century, largely because of Freudianism, there grew a strong conception that there is someone inside us, the "true" us, who is not allowed to reveal itself. We see a philanthropist and theorize that he gives money to charities not because he is good, but because he needs the attention his cold parents never gave him or because he needs a tax deduction. We see a carjacker and theorize he acts this way because he grew up in a loveless home, humiliated by his poverty. Regardless of psychological or sociological causes for certain behaviors, we cannot read minds. We look for indications in the speech or other behaviors of a person that these causes are indeed behind the more overt behavior.

CHOICES

One way of looking at character is to see that the plot presents a series of choices to the characters. Each choice further refines our sense of who the character is. In a well-made plot, each choice in the progression from beginning to end also increases the danger or cost to the main character. In the series of scenes that compose *Oedipus the King*, Oedipus is confronted with a problem, usually to find out some piece of information which will lead him closer to discovering who killed King Laius and brought a curse upon the city. Each step draws him closer and closer to himself and along the way a number of characters warn him that he shouldn't pursue this quest. We learn who Oedipus is because he refuses to back down even when he finally has the intuition it would be safer if he did. At one point, his wife Jocasta (unknown to him as also his mother) realizes where the investigation is leading. She urges him to stop, saying he doesn't need to know the truth. It is enough that *she* knows. Much has been made of the implications in that remark. Is she willing to live with the secret that she has unknowingly married her son? Has she already decided to kill herself and merely wants to spare him the dreadful facts of his birth? Her words hint at aspects of her character that have provoked much discussion among readers and especially among those performing the play.

It is hard to imagine an effective plot whose protagonist will not, like Oedipus, pursue the goal to the end, whether it is bitter or sweet. Certainly in life there are many people who are acted upon by circumstances and events, continuing to flow with whatever tide comes along. But main characters, in order to engage a reader, must be at least slightly exaggerated. They must be willing to do more than ordinary people, be cleverer or tougher or more incorruptible or more feeling or more angry or more incompetent. The way their traits are demonstrated is, as I've said, by throwing them in the skillet and turning on the heat.

It is commonplace to hear writers proclaim that they had a plot and when they got to a certain point the character came to life and refused to do what it was supposed to. This is all hocus-pocus. You are the writer. Characters only "live" in the imagination. They do not have an independent existence. The character will do what you make it do. If it seems wrong for the character to do a certain thing, then the character has been created wrong or the plot took a wrong turn which violated its internal logic.

Suppose we outline a plot in which our protagonist Amelia falls in love with Hugo and is about to be married to him. Her sister Bedelia also loves Hugo.

Now suppose that in the early part of the novel, we show Bedelia being aggressive and determined. She arranges to "bump into" Hugo on the campus and invite him to coffee. She finds clever ways to keep Amelia and Hugo from having much time alone. We see a number of instances in which she shows a genuine hatred for her sister, and we wonder if she is trying to take Hugo away out of jealousy. Hugo has no real idea what she is up to. He considers her a harmless flirt and thinks he likes her because she is, in a number of ways, like her sister, who is also resourceful and clever. He's flattered by her attention, but the day of the wedding rehearsal, when she expresses her true feelings, he is flummoxed, flees from the vicar's office into the garden, and pretends to Amelia that he was suddenly ill. Everyone ascribes it to nerves.

But Bedelia decides to kill herself over him. She does. On the wedding day the other bridesmaids go to fetch her. She is found hanging from her balcony wearing Amelia's wedding dress. This ruins the planned wedding, of course, and drives a wedge between Hugo and Amelia, as Amelia believes that Hugo may have led Bedelia on.

Your plot is moving along fine, you think, but then, when you read over your manuscript you see that Bedelia, as she was drawn in the earlier chapters, would never kill herself. She is far too enterprising, far too crafty to resort to the ultimate way out. No, she would concoct another scheme. She would engineer another plan to prove to Hugo that he actually loves her, not her fastidious sister Amelia. If Bedelia kills herself, the reader will find it merely another contrived plot device intended to drive a wedge between Amelia and Hugo.

What a pickle you've gotten yourself into, though! What a splendid bit of spectacle the discovery of Bedelia's suicide would be! In Amelia's stolen wedding dress she would dangle from the balcony, twisting slowly in the wind. The bridesmaid would shriek! Amelia and Bedelia's father would come running and cry out in anguish. Amelia would throw herself against Hugo and faint. The gardener would come running with his ladder to cut Bedelia down, and then, when it is realized she is dead, they would see the note pinned to her chest, her last bit of revenge. "I GAVE MYSELF TO HUGO IN LIFE; HE SHALL BE MINE IN DEATH." Hugo is baffled and asks what it could mean, but the cold stares of the wedding party say what everyone thinks.

You'd hate to get rid of this scene! You really loved it from the moment you conceived it in all its operatic splendor. It was the inspiration for the entire book, you say. But Bedelia is just not right for suicide. If things stand as they are, you book may seem contrived, silly. Bedelia hanging herself will seem to be for your motivations rather than her own. Would your book be better without it?

That depends, of course, on what type of novel you're writing, Obviously you cannot let things stand as they are. The two most important elements of your novel are not in harmony. You have three choices here: change the character, change the plot, or throw up your hands and write a different novel.

If you want to be a novelist, the third possibility is not an option. Even if you cannot solve a problem, you must continue to wrestle with it. It will teach you much about yourself and your writing, even if you do not reach a satisfying solution. In many instances, a brilliant answer (or at least an adequate one) may pop into your head when you're showering or dozing off in the hammock. I have many story ideas filed in my brain's attic which I've never quite been able to work out, but I may get them right yet. I have many short stories and a couple of novels in print because I did not give up on what seemed an insoluble problem. If you quit faced with problems, and rush off to pursue "better" ideas, well, you'll end up with a drawer of unfinished manuscripts.

ADJUSTING CHARACTER TO SUIT THE PLOT

So, then, for us there are only two choices in our melodramatic scenario. One is to change Bedelia. The other is to change the scene. Changing Bedelia will mean revising her character from the book's beginning. This will be a lot of work, but whoever said writing a novel was easy? You will need to revise scenes so that the reader gets hints of a character who would turn to such a flamboyant and cruel way of committing suicide. How, in everyday moments, can you show this without giving away the outcome? As much as possible in a novel, we want to do this in scenes. We want to show, instead of tell.

Perhaps you'll have an ordinary scene in which the sisters are having breakfast, and Bedelia could react to a routine disappointment in a way that implies her extreme tendencies. There wasn't enough corn meal for spoon bread, which is her favorite dish for breakfast. Perhaps the sisters' father announces that the estate is not doing well this year and Amelia and Bedelia will have to postpone finishing school until the next harvest. Amelia is disappointed, but Bedelia goes into a blue funk. The characters are thus contrasted and Bedelia's depressive tendencies are shown, although they don't seem serious at that point.

Perhaps we see an evening soirée in which various guests are playing the card game whist by candlelight. This could be a fine scene, giving you a chance to show the sisters' social class interacting. What happens when Bedelia loses a close game? When Bedelia moves around the room, are there hints of her desperation to be loved more than her sister is? Perhaps she tries to interject witty remarks into other people's conversations, but her jokes are never quite clever enough. Does she find pretenses to interrupt Amelia and Hugo when they walk out alone on the veranda? At that point it might seem like she is merely a nuisance. Later we will see that it was a sign of deep-seated problems.

Throughout the passage of the novel from its beginning to Bedelia's death, you must drop hints that reveal Bedelia's future without making them too obvious. It's a tough balancing act which requires writing skill, but do not shy away from a challenge. You cannot become better unless you try to be better. Failing is learning, but if you work hard enough you will succeed in ways you never imagined you could. Bedelia (like all of the characters) must participate in events which make her consistent, lifelike, and capable of doing what she does. She must also be a person who, if the readers don't sympathize with her, they must at least understand her.

ADJUST PLOT TO REFLECT CHARACTER

Ruthlessness with your own text is a requirement for being an effective novelist. Perhaps instead of changing the character, you change the plot. Okay, so you thought it would be a great scene. As you created Bedelia in the previous pages, she became someone you didn't anticipate, but who you now find much more clear and interesting than your original conception. If it's already completed, put it in your file cabinet. If the scene doesn't work in this story, perhaps it will work in another. Grit your teeth and firmly escort it out of the novel.

Now, of course, you have a gaping hole in your novel. At this point, your plot had gone 1) Amelia accepts Hugo's proposal and the wedding is arranged, 2) Bedelia in despair and jealousy of her sister, hangs herself on the day of the wedding, and 3) Hugo is unjustly accused of being the cause of Bedelia's death, and he and Amelia are estranged. Unless you've decided that it is better for Hugo and Amelia to marry and for Bedelia to go on scheming in some different way, you'll need a number 2) that causes the wedding to be cancelled and leads to the couple's separation. 1) must cause 2) and 2) must cause 3).

We decided that the novel before scene 1) shows us that Bedelia is clever and tricky. Therefore, whatever she does in scene 2), should reflect that. She might (to borrow one of Shakespeare's favorite ploys) arrange for Amelia to overhear a conversation that isn't what it appears to be. She might arrange to have something about Hugo revealed that makes him seem fraudulent. She forges a document alleging he never legally divorced his wife in Jamaica. A strange man turns up at the house (bribed by Amelia) who alleges Hugo had a bevy of native women as his consorts in the West Indies. She slips into his bedroom the night before the wedding, pretending in the dark to be Amelia and making certain to be "discovered" by the maid in the morning. Or perhaps the weak-willed Hugo (if that is how he is characterized) is simply seduced by her.

Whatever is chosen must irrevocably alter what follows. Is Amelia aware of the particular trick used by Bedelia? In some of the above plots she might not. In some of them, Bedelia's deception might even be concealed from the reader. The reader might believe that Hugo has lied, but subsequent events reveal that he is the victim of Bedelia's scheming. Hugo would have to be portrayed in such a way as to make belief in his deception possible, but not so definitely that the revelation that he is a victim would seem like a *deus ex machina* coercing a happy ending.

Different choices will result in different paths through the rest of the novel. When a plot is properly created with its chain of causality, nothing in it can be altered without affecting other parts. Like when a pebble hits a pond or a massive meteor crashes into in the ocean, ripples will radiate in all directions through the plot. You must make certain that they enhance, rather than destroy the desired effect, and whether you change the plot to accommodate the character or change the character to accommodate the plot, you may need to do extensive revision.

THE PATCH

Sometimes in novels you can detect what I call "the patch." This is a term borrowed from the software business. You buy expensive and complicated software, and more often than not, it has minor flaws in the program. Perhaps in a game the sound cuts off when the virtual airplane you are flying does a loop. Perhaps in a word processing program when you zoom in on a particular sized page, the page numbers get fouled up. Once the designers become aware of this program through furious customer complaints, they send you a "patch" to fix the problem. Big programs often have dozens of patches. They are intended to solve the problem until the next version comes out. When the engineers design the next version, they will attempt to repair the problem in the program as a whole.

One mistake of beginning and less talented writers is a reliance upon patching rather than good design. Let's go back to our previous example. You come to the point that it doesn't make sense for Bedelia to commit suicide. As I said earlier, you face the choice of changing either the plot or the character. Both involve revision to solve the fundamental flaw. Ah, you decide, it isn't that big a deal. You decide that Bedelia, although she has been resourceful throughout her life, the emotion of this problem overwhelms her, driving her to suicidal despair. You produce a paragraph around the point of Bedelia's suicide which explains this. You don't need to rework the whole novel. You've made a patch.

A patch is very much like a *deus ex machina*. It drops into the story out of nowhere and forces things to go where the author wants them, not where they would go naturally. The patch is also as convincing as most gods out of a machine: not at all. It reminds me once again of Anton Chekhov's dictum about the gun on the mantlepiece. If it's hanging there, it's got to be fired. But, by implication, Chekhov is also saying that for a gun to be fired, it should be hanging there for a while.

A patch is little different than having your character suddenly "remember" something she can use to get her out of a jam. The fact that a character had a chemistry set when she was a little girl and blew out her kitchen windows might be introduced early in a novel. Later, locked in the evildoer's basement, she might concoct an explosive to get the cellar door opened. If the chemistry set story had not been earlier introduced, it would seem ridiculous that she suddenly remembers how to make an explosive out of coal and naphtha. It would seem like the author is trying to patch a problem that he hadn't been smart enough to consider in creating the novel.

Curiously sometimes beginning authors ruminate on their novels until they see problems which no reader who is enjoying the book would think of. In motion picture history, there is a story about Michael Curtis, most successful as director of *Casablanca*. In another film, he suddenly ordered the prop men to take a piano out of the background of an indoor scene. The cinematographer went ballistic. If they took

Mastering Plot

the piano out, they would have to reshoot every scene in which the piano appeared. Curtis allegedly said, "Take it out. If they're watching the piano, they're not watching the movie." When the film appeared, the cinematographer went to the theater. No one in the audience seemed disturbed by the disappearing piano.

Now this story about a master director tells us something important as writers. It is easy to become obsessed with details that do not actually affect the forward movement of the story. For example, I have seen many beginning writers get so wrapped up in explaining how a character got from one place to another that the compelling reason for the journey got lost. In another instance, a character was mugged and lost consciousness when he had only two hours to get somewhere. Evidently it occurred to the writer that the muggers probably would have taken his Rolex. The writer then inserted (or seemed to have inserted) a paragraph explaining how lucky the man was that he had taken off his Rolex while washing his hands. It was still deep in his briefcase. He had only fifteen minutes to stop the terrorists!

All of this was a very elaborate patch for no reason. The character needed to know the time. Or maybe he didn't really—but assuming he did, there are a million easier ways to solve this problem than with this unlikely patch.

Patching a character has a similar unnatural feel. The author gets a notion that a character's behavior needs to be justified and creates a passage to do so. Whop! It's slapped on the story like a poster on a telephone pole. The desperation of the author shows through and both the plot and the character become artificial.

BRAINSTORMER #10

Character is as character does. But what does a character do to reveal inner qualities?

Take each of the following abstract remarks and give two concrete examples of outward actions to reveal the trait. In this exercise, do not use dialog by other characters as an action (i.e. "Jane, you ridiculous slut!").

For example:

1) Ebenezer Scrooge was a parsimonious miser.
   A) He eats a disgusting warmed over soup for his Christmas Eve dinner.
   B) He treats two well-meaning charity solicitors with contempt, telling them that the poor deserve to be in the workhouses.

Try these:

2) Joe hated dogs.
3) Karen was afraid of flying
4) Antonio was a good child.
5) Carlton was an unmannered wretch.
6) Emily was a classy woman, but also miserly.
7) Jason was depressed.
8) Toni had an IQ of 175.
9) Cecilia was sociopathic. She felt nothing for other people.
10) Lelia was nervous.

Look at your answers and judge them harshly. How many were the first things that came to mind? How many do you remember having seen in some other book or context, such as television?

On television, people often show they are nervous by pacing. Because of this, when the audience sees or the readers reads of a person pacing, it doesn't so much reveal nervousness in the character as it does laziness in the writer.

Reject all those on your list that seem obvious or that you have seen before. There will be many. Do better ones, but make certain that each less obvious one is also clear.

When you're writing, do this exercise with your characters and you will be creating actions for your plot.

Chapter 10
Plots Ready-Made

Once, while haunting a dusty used-book store, I stumbled across a decaying set of books called *The Plot Genie* by Wycliffe A. Hill. It was published by the Ernest E. Gagnon Company of Hollywood, California in multiple volumes in the 1930s. It promised to provide an infinite set of plots for whoever might employ its methods. It was conveniently divided into the popular genres of its day, and included volumes entitled the *Short-short Story*, *Detective Mystery*, *Western*, *Science Fiction*, *Confession* stories, and so on. The volume on comedy was the largest, perhaps illustrating the difficulty of mechanizing humor.

Hill's books consisted of a formula for the kind of story that magazines of each genre were buying then, an explanation of that formula, and many pages of potential variations to be used in creating the stories. With the books came some sort of wheel that the aspiring author could spin to randomly select these elements. For example, the first element in the detective story is the protagonist. Who is the detective? Spin Wycliffe A. Hill's wheel and you might come up with any one of 180 different occupations conveniently listed by Hill. Your detective might be an aviator, a millionaire, a chemist, a movie star, a dog breeder, a farmer, a man of the cloth, an entrepreneur, a janitor, a college professor, or any one of dozens of other possibilities. Hill's choices often reflected their era. One choice for a female character was "an aviatrix." One choice for a villain was "a Shylock." The choices for various elements of the science fiction stories were equally as dated: ray-guns, atomic spaceships, and "wizened fiends" for villains.

Also included were lists of locales, motivations, harrowing situations, predicaments, climaxes, and other aspects of a story. Locales in the short-short book included number 4, "In an Abbey"; number 11, "In a love nest"; number 128, "In a dope den"; and number 180, "In a flotilla." Motivations included, "Desire to suppress a fraud," "Desire to crush a rival," and "To save one from a disastrous marriage." Climaxes included, "It develops that a dangerous enemy is only a mad man," "Escape is effected by a novel means of signaling," and "In which the villain does his work so well that it reacts favorably to the hero."

Hill must have spent years making his lists and it all seemed a bit ridiculous to me. After all, if would-be writers can't come up with an interesting character or a dramatic situation, perhaps they should head down to the pool hall and improve their skills at eight-ball.

But, don't rush to judgment. Blow the dust and the aviatrixes off the *Plot Genie* and you'll see that Wycliffe A. Hill—whoever he was—was on to something. What seems so archaically hokey actually works pretty well. If we look at his formula for the Western story for example, it hardly seems exciting. It consists of eleven elements: 1) locale, 2) hero, 3) girl, 4) villain, 5) cause of conflict, 6) villain's scheme against hero, 7) hero's method of thwarting the villain, 8)a counter action by the villain, 9)a test between hero and villain, 10) the critical situation or jeopardy, and 11) the hero wins when.

However, if you take *High Noon*, often called the first adult Western and a classic of moviemaking, we find a nearly precise correspondence between Hill's plot elements and the film. There are interesting twists on elements, such as there is a second "girl" and the villain doesn't actually appear on screen until 9)the test. With Hill's formula and a little tweaking, you've got *Unforgiven* or *Shane*. Change the locale to a mining colony on a moon of Jupiter in the future, and the plot of *High Noon* becomes *Outland*, a film made in 1981.

Some plot structures are, it seems, inherently effective. In another used book store I found the 1929 *Plotto: The Master Book of All Plots* by William Wallace Cook. Stapled in the front was a typed letter from *Writer's Digest* editor Richard K. Abbott explaining how to use it.

Plotto resurfaced recently in a slightly updated form available for the computer. Writer's Digest now offers an excellent book by Ronald B. Tobias called *20 Master Plots and How to Build Them*—no wheels to spin, no aviatrixes.

All of this may have been started by Johann Wolfgang von Goethe, the great German author, who reported once that Carlo Gozzi (a minor Italian author who died in 1809) had once argued there were only 36 plots in all of literature. Neither of them, however, wrote them down. Gérard de Nerval, a French poet, later listed 24, but an obscure scholar named Georges Polti (born in 1868, he now has a web site devoted to him) wrote a popular book which confirmed there were exactly 36 plots. This led a movie mogul to say, "Yes, but only six of them are box office." That remark probably explains why we see such little variation in the basic plots of movies each year. If you're going to spend 10 to 200 million dollars on a film, you'll feel a lot more comfortable with a plot you know has worked well in the past.

The great thing about Hill's wheel and lists was that it forced the mind to pair up unconventional things. If we were to make up a Western, we'd likely lean heavily of other Westerns we've seen or read. The main character is a sheriff in conflict with an evil cattle baron. The baron insults the sheriff in a saloon. And so on. By spinning the wheel, you might get a sheriff who is a Russian Jewish immigrant, and the bad guy is a dwarf who is a bootlegger. The bootlegger insults the sheriff in a public bathhouse. Already, the imagination is running. The story comes to life because of totally new feeling the writer and then the reader will get from these odd conjunctions.

But the plots are the same. How uncreative! you protest.

But so what? The plot is the foundation upon which we build our stories. Very different houses may be built on similar foundations. A solid structure means a solid house, regardless of the shapes of the window panes or the shape of the balusters. It isn't just the Devil that's in the details, there's also the creativity.

But if I use the same plot over and over, I'll be boring! you say. Really? First of all, readers enjoy a good story, but they're not generally interested in how it was made. Most people don't worry about how their flatscreen makes images or how penicillin cures their sore throat. They're just happy these things work. With a novel, most readers want to laugh, cry, and think about the content. Those who do bother to analyze it may even enjoy the fact that you've cleverly reused a previously existing plot.

Look at any series author. Writers of mystery and thriller series often worry about the possibility of repeating themselves, but the variations they use in plot are usually not as great as those in the details. Charlie Chan at the opera. Charlie Chan on a cruise ship. Charlie Chan in Egypt. I pointed out in detail in a small book I published some years ago that Dick Francis, who has had a bestseller every year since 1981, uses a formula based on the type of character, setting, and other elements. In a sense, he is not a series author because he does not repeat his main character very often. In most novels, he creates a whole new set of characters, somehow involved with the world of horse-racing. Though there is a lot of resemblance in the characterization of his protagonists, the fact that his books continue to be best sellers is a sign that readers prefer the similarities from book to book. It's like visiting an old friend who is a gourmet. You never know what dish he's going to cook, but you know it's going to be served in style.

THE SIMPLEST FORMULA

As mentioned before, there have been many attempts to catalog all of the possible effective plots. Perhaps the simplest is this. There are only two plots: 1) someone goes on a journey, or 2) a stranger comes to town. If we think about these, we can probably find no fiction which wouldn't fall into one of the two categories. *The Odyssey,* obviously, is among those in the first category. *Oscar and Lucinda*, the Booker Prize novel by Australian Peter Carey, features a clergyman who takes a glass church to Australia. *Lolita* is mostly Humbert Humbert's attempt to escape with the girl. How many novels revolve around a character's spiritual journey? The interior landscape can be a larger world than the earthly one, but often the spiritual jouney is combined with a physical one, as in John Bunyan's *Pilgrim's Progress* or Hermann Hesse's *Siddhartha*.

The stranger coming to town is actually only a change of point of view from the journey category, because, after all, the stranger is on a journey or he wouldn't be coming to town. In Virgil's *Aeneid*, Troy is sacked and Aeneas sails around the Mediterranean looking for a place to rebuild his life. He comes to Carthage, where he meets Dido and falls in love with her. If we tell the story from Aeneas' point of view we have the first category of story. If we tell it from Dido's point of view, we have the second. Could we, therefore, reduce our two types of plot into only one? We could say, "There is only one plot. In it there is movement (Aristotle's use of the word *action*) and a change of circumstance."

But how useful is reducing all stories to this? It might help us to understand how existing stories work, but how will it help us create new ones? It's hard to imagine that Mark Twain's writing "The Man That Corrupted Hadleyburg" began with his wanting to write about a stranger coming to town or that Arthur Conan Doyle began forming *The Hound of the Baskervilles* by thinking he'd like to send Sherlock Holmes on a trip. There's not enough in these two categories to get the creative juices flowing in most of us.

I don't want to assert that too definitively since creativity flows from unpredictably myriad sources. You know that already from the way you get ideas out of nowhere, don't you? It happens to everybody—it's just that writers pay more attention to those little inspirational nudges. A fragment of conversation, the sight of a woman on the street, or an old song on the radio may get any of us going. That detail combined with the journey or stranger motif might lead somewhere. Tony Hillerman, the world-renowned mystery writer, likens this process to being a street person who wanders around picking up strange objects and putting them into his shopping cart because he thinks the objects might be useful in some indeterminate way in the future. Here's an odd character I'd like to write about, you'll say. What kind of plot would she make sense in?

The creativity in Wycliffe Hill's books did not actually come from plotting, as I said earlier, but from placing various "found" things in random juxtaposition. It's not all that different from the Surrealist dictum that "Beauty is the meeting of a sewing machine and an umbrella on an operating table." Hill just made the umbrellas and operating tables easy to find. But the plot formula did not change.

ANOTHER WAY OF LOOKING AT FORMULA PLOTTING

There is a more serious way of looking at Hill's pulp fiction method which doesn't make it seem quite as cheesy. When Europeans began spreading—and often imposing—their culture to the furthest reaches of the globe, some of them began recording the mythology and legend of alien peoples. Often, they were quite surprised by the resemblance among certain myths. At first they assumed that some original story, such as that of the great flood which destroys humankind, started in one location and spread outward. However, this seemed very unlikely in certain instances when there was no other indication of any contact between two different peoples. Could a tribe on a remote island in a Pacific archipelago have gotten the flood story of ancient Sumer from Bronze Age travelers? Possibly, but it seemed doubtful.

James Frasier cataloged mythical resemblances in his thick book, *The Golden Bough*, and later Carl Gustav Jung developed the theory of the collective unconscious. Humans, he said, all go through identical life cycles. "Man is born of woman and dies," says the King James Bible. We eat, we bleed, we learn society's rules, we seek shelter and companionship, and so on. It would be logical, therefore, that all of us would have much in common, that myths about the quest for immortality would recur across the globe. That fear of nature's destructive force would turn itself into fear of supernatural powers and into a God or gods who would wipe out mankind for being disobedient. Certain myths would reflect the collective unconscious and be evocative to every culture.

Do you see where I'm going? Certain plots will work better than others because, in some mysterious way, they make contact with this collective unconscious. Or perhaps certain plots work well because they resemble other plots which we were nurtured by. A Christian boy or girl is taught the story of Joseph in Egypt. This is a sacred story of great meaning, and thereafter, as the children grow they measure other stories against this one, finding pleasure when later stories work in the same way.

Whether Jung is right or it is just a matter of training is merely an intellectual question for those of us who want to write a good novel. What's important about it is that there are certain plots which have great appeal. These sure-fire plots can be used to make the novel each of us wants to write be instantly more appealing. Joseph Campbell (in *The Hero with a Thousand Faces* and several other books) drew on Jung to argue that the heroic plot in most cultures followed the same pattern. Later, Christopher Vogler drew on Joseph Campbell to create a method for plotting motion pictures. No one seemed to have noticed that the mysterious Wycliffe A. Hill (and others before him) had done this favor for writers earlier, by reducing published genre stories to their basic plots. These are what the Detective-Action story consists of, said Hill. Do it and you'll sell Detective-Action stories.

We all know it's not as simple as that. The problem is that after you've got your plot worked out, you've still got to write the story. As I pointed out earlier in the book, a few stupid sentences and your story will look stupid, regardless of the quality of the plot. Once again, readers will admire your story, but do not usually give much thought to plot. If the plotting is poor, they will just know that something is horribly wrong.

USING PRE-EXISTING PLOTS

Now can you see why using pre-existing plots makes sense? You will probably be doing it anyway, without realizing it. My first novel, *The Murder of Frau Schütz* concerns a German officer who investigates the murder of the commandant's wife in a concentration camp. He goes on a journey to the camp, interviews suspects, and finds the murderer. In truth, when I wrote it, I did not think of it as a mystery, though I knew it had mystery elements. When it was nominated for the Edgar Allan Poe prize, I was somewhat astounded at my own myopia.

Of course it is a mystery! It resembles, in certain respects, hundreds of other books in the genre. Initially this bothered me. I thought I hadn't been as creative as I imagined, but then I saw the pleasure the book had given others. I was told how original it was. I was asked where I had come up with such an original idea. Gradually, I began to understand. One of the reasons the book was successful was the underlying familiar structure.

One night my wife and I were watching *Night of the Generals*, a motion picture starring Peter O'Toole and Omar Sharif. My wife said, "This is like *Frau Schütz*." I indignantly protested it wasn't. Yet, a reviewer in a major newspaper compared my book to the novel by Hans Hellmut Kirst. Of course there was a resemblance. *Night of the Generals* is about the investigation of a murder in Nazi Germany, and underlying it is also the detective plot which has worked so well for so many writers. Now, I am happy to admit there is a resemblance between my book and Kirst's. It means I was doing something right. I did it in my way and he did it in his, but we were both playing the same game.

We're not talking plagiarism. Plagiarism is appropriating someone else's work and claiming it for your own. Plots, stripped of the elements which make them stories, are structures. No one has a patent on the parallelogram. Comedian Allan Sherman once tried to patent the key of C in music because no one had. That is as big a joke as patenting a plot.

Nothing is more tedious than when English professors argue who invented the detective plot, for example. Was it Edgar Allan Poe? Was it the anonymous author of *Bel and the Dragon*, an ancient Hebrew narrator? Neither Poe nor the ancient author used the term "detective." Anna Katherine Green, a pioneer of the modern mystery, is credited with that. But the plot was always there. Poe may never have read *Bel and the Dragon*. How could he be accused of plagiarizing it? Green's stories are very different from Poe's. She was no plagiarist.

BRAINSTORMER #11

1) Make a list of ten books that have always meant a lot to you. Don't be a snob. They don't have to be certified "Great Books of the Western World" or any other world. They can be books that affected you deeply, but might be considered guilty pleasures. They are the books you enjoyed. You don't want to write *War and Peace* or *Middlemarch,* anyway, right? But you might want to write something like *Beau Geste, Hound of the Baskervilles,* or *The Girl With the Dragon Tattoo.* The first few books will probably spring to mind easily, but the last few might be harder.

Lay the list in front of you and see if there is anything in common among these books. Are six of them historical mysteries or stories of women in jeopardy or children's books with an occult aspect? Do most of the books feature a particular kind of character, such as Native American policemen, the very rich, spies, or independent women in business?

You should be getting a sense from this list of the kind of book you prefer and have often read. If you've often liked a particular type of book, you are probably better suited to write such a book. Your mind may be predisposed to the assumptions implicit in such a book. If you like horror, you must believe in the supernatural. If you can fantasize yourself going up a dark alley in pursuit of a purse snatcher, perhaps you'd be good at police procedurals.

Cross out the books that don't have anything in common with each other. Look at the ones that are left. Pick out the one you think is the best and do a briefly worded story outline, such as this:

1) A woman astronaut, lost in space and desperate for food, lands on an unexplored planet.
2) She finds the descendants of a family stranded seventy years ago.

3) As she gets ready for bed, the handsome son knocks on her door and attempts to seduce her. She feels uneasy and resists. He quietly leaves.

And so on.

When you reach the end of your outline, get another legal pad or open up a second window on your word processor and write a parallel outline, inverting things or reversing elements. For example:

1) A Martian eunuch has a problem with fuel leakage. He docks at the nearest space station.
2) The workers there are all androids, all identical, and are totally indifferent to his presence.
3) As he rests in one of the guest chambers, one of the androids attacks him with a knife. He beats off the attack, but the android escapes

And so on.

You can see how different your new version is immediately, though it is completely following the pattern of the other book. You are using the other book as a model to create something original, but the underlying structure is the same. To make a good novel out of it might require additional adjustments, but if the original book was well structured, your altered one should be as well. Motivations, settings, characters, and so forth can be totally different with the underlying plot nearly identical.

BRAINSTORMER #12

Choose a story from mythology, legend, classic literature, or religion. Briefly outline its plot. Take each step of the plot and reset it to a different setting and time.

For example, you might take the story of Abraham and Isaac, in which God asks Abraham to prove his loyalty by sacrificing his son. Could the story be changed so that it takes place in Chicago in the

1930s? Abraham becomes Charlie Koper, a fireman. His son by a previous marriage is suspected of serial arson. Charlie is pressured by the police to help them catch his son before he burns another building.

Or suppose you take the story of Hamlet and set it in a corporation. Or suppose you take the Norse myth of Baldur and reset it in the Civil War. Some of these won't produce good results, but you'll be surprised how many will. A real author wouldn't do this! you protest. Oh yeah? Take a look at Jane Smiley's novel *A Thousand Acres*. It's based on *King Lear*, which is itself based on a Celtic myth retold by Geoffrey of Monmouth. Take a look at John Cheever's "Metamorphoses," modernizing stories found in the Roman poet Ovid's *Metamorphoses*. And remember our old friend William Shakespeare. Only two or three of his plays seem to be based upon original material, and one of them, *Titus Andronicus*, is utterly appalling.

Final Thoughts

Plotting isn't all there is in creating an adequate novel, but it is much more important than many people acknowledge. Some people worry about other aspects of the novel more, but already have an instinct for plotting which has been acquired through reading and imitation. Others need to meticulously work at their plots. But all of us need to pay attention to it. I hope after all these pages that you've acquired some useful insights into the process.

All writers need to find their own best ways of working. Some of us do better in the early light of dawn; others prosper in the dark. Some use the best computer money can buy; others still use a yellow legal pad and pencil. Some write a small number of hours each day; others spend weeks without writing and then work twenty hour days for two weeks. There are no real rules about these kinds of things. You need to figure out what works best for you and then stick to it. As the old saying attributed to Alexandre Dumas goes: "Nothing succeeds like success."

When I began this book, I told you I would not give you "the secret" to plotting. Depending on your way of looking at it, there are many secrets or there are none. Some people are cured by an antibiotic, others are killed by it. What I hope to have helped you with is your ability to think about plot, to exercise control over your plots and to use them to your best advantage. I want you to find out what works best for you in telling the kind of story you want to tell. I don't want you to write like me. I don't want you to follow my advice without questioning it and without testing it. Then if you come to agree with what I have learned about plotting by my own reading, teaching, and writing, and passed on to you, it will be a living and useful toolbox, instead of a memorized concept. You will be able to create a book that gives pleasure.

Remember, writing is a way of life. If you're not writing, you're not a writer. I can't teach you to write well. Only you can do that. Try to develop that peculiar schizophrenia which can be so useful to writers: the ability to read your own writings as if you've never seen them before. And do something even harder than describing the indescribable: judge yourself harshly, but fairly.

Enough advice! Stop making excuses and get to work! Plot!

Manufactured by Amazon.ca
Acheson, AB